Feasts of Faith

Sept 14, 2008
Feast of the Cross

Dear Nick —

Peace + Blessings!

Bill

Other books published by the Orthodox Research Institute include:

William C. Mills. *From Pascha to Pentecost: Reflections on the Gospel of John*

William C. Mills. *Prepare O Bethlehem: Reflections on the Scripture Readings for the Christmas-Epiphany Season*

William C. Mills. *Baptize All Nations: Reflections on the Gospel of Matthew for the Pentecost Season*

Sebastian Dabovich. *Preaching in the Orthodox Church: Lectures and Sermons by a Priest of the Holy Orthodox Church*

Protopresbyter George Dion. Dragas. *Ecclesiasticus I: Introducing Eastern Orthodoxy*

Protopresbyter George Dion. Dragas. *Ecclesiasticus II: Orthodox Icons, Saints, Feasts and Prayer*

Protopresbyter George Dion. Dragas. *The Lord's Prayer according to Saint Makarios of Corinth*

Protopresbyter George Dion. Dragas. *Saint Athanasius of Alexandria: Original Research and New Perspectives*

Protopresbyter George Dion. Dragas. *St. Cyril of Alexandria's Teaching on the Priesthood*

Alphonse and Rachel Goettmann. *The Power of the Name: The History and Practices of the Jesus Prayer*

Alphonse and Rachel Goettmann. *The Spiritual Wisdom and Practices of Early Christianity*

Archimandrite Laurence Mancuso. *Being Good — Responding to Our Faith: Notes from a Poor Monk*

Matthew the Poor. *The Titles of Christ*

Protopresbyter John S. Romanides. *An Outline of Orthodox Patristic Dogmatics*, in Greek and English. Edited and translated by Protopresbyter George Dion. Dragas

FEASTS OF FAITH

Reflections on
the Major Feast Days

William C. Mills

ORTHODOX
RESEARCH
INSTITUTE

Rollinsford, New Hampshire

Published by Orthodox Research Institute
20 Silver Lane
Rollinsford, NH 03869
www.orthodoxresearchinstitute.org

Library of Congress Control Number: 2008934942

ISBN 978-1-933275-23-9

PRAYER BEFORE THE GOSPEL

(*From the Divine Liturgy of Saint John Chrysostom*)

Illumine our hearts O Master who loves mankind, with the pure light of Thy divine knowledge. Open the eyes of our mind to the understanding of Thy gospel teachings. Implant also in us the fear of Thy blessed commandments, that, trampling down all carnal desires, we may enter upon a spiritual manner of living, both thinking and doing such things as are well pleasing unto Thee. For Thou art the illumination of our souls and bodies, O Christ our God, and unto Thee we ascribe glory, together with Thy Father, who is from everlasting, and Thine all-holy, good, and life-creating Spirit, now and ever and unto ages of ages. Amen.

TABLE OF CONTENTS

INTRODUCTION

The Orthodox liturgical year includes twelve major feast days that commemorate special events in the life of both Jesus Christ and the Virgin Mary the Theotokos. We celebrate Jesus' birth at Christmas, His baptism at Epiphany, as well as His entry into Jerusalem on Palm Sunday. Likewise, we recall Mary's birth at the feast of her Nativity in September as well as her death during the feast of her Dormition or Falling Asleep in August. These feast days are liturgical sign-posts throughout the year directing us towards Pascha or the Lord's Resurrection which is referred to in the Church year as the "feast of feasts"—the central most celebration of the year—the death and resurrection of Jesus. These twelve feast days, in addition to Pascha, are constant reminders about celebrating the life that God has given us in His Son Jesus.

In addition to the major or great feasts of the Church, there are what are called minor or lesser feasts, such as St. Nicholas on December 6, the Circumcision of our Lord on January 1, the Protection of the Theotokos on October 1, the feast of Sts. Peter and Paul on June 29, and the Synaxis of the Angels on November 8. Depending on the local practice some of these minor feasts days may or may not be celebrated in the local worshipping community. As with the major feast days, the minor feast days also include specially prescribed Scripture readings as well as special liturgical hymnography. *Feasts of Faith* only includes reflections on the major feast days, however, the reader is encouraged to learn more about the lesser feast days on your own.

Because feast days are very special the Church celebrates these events with splendor. In some parishes the festal icon, usually decorated with flowers or fresh greenery, is placed in the center of the Church for veneration by the faithful. Sometimes during great festal celebrations, such as Christmas or Pascha, the entire Church is decorated literally "from top to bottom" with flowers and greenery on the icons, on the icon stands, and on the icon screen or *iconostasis*. Also, clergy and altar servers wear different colored vestments depending on the particular celebration and the choir sings special hymns commemorating the feast. Some feasts such as Palm Sunday or Pascha include processions around the Church. Other feasts such as Epiphany may include a procession to a lake or river in order to bless water.

Likewise, many feast days include special prayers for blessings. Grapes and fruit are blessed at the feast of the Transfiguration and flowers and seeds are blessed at the feast of the Dormition of Mary. We bless candles at the feast of the Meeting of the Lord and palms and pussy willows at the feast of Palm Sunday. These blessings are important parts of our life and are small ways that we remember that everything in creation is worthy of a blessing and that all things come from God Himself. I vividly remember my parents bringing a bowl of fruit to be blessed at Transfiguration and fresh cut flowers from our garden for a blessing at Dormition. These memories are some of the most memorable ones that I have from Church life. This is also a case in point that children do learn from their experiences in Church, experiencing various blessings, lighting candles, kissing icons, eating bread and wine, and so forth. The material nature of our faith, celebrated throughout the year in these feast days, are constant reminders that the material world is indeed created by God and worthy of a blessing.

Feast days are ways that Orthodox Christians celebrate our common life in Christ, our communal remembrance of God's salvation. The late Orthodox theologian, pastor, and professor Alexander Schmemann comments on the importance of feast days by saying:

> Why not instead reflect more deeply, and ask why it was that for
> centuries and for literally millions of people, it was the Church
> year which sanctified them and gave meaning to their lives?
> Why not try to understand the wonderfully organic fabric of

feasts, which we weave for each season in its own unique color, its own unique depth? The light of Christmas, the bright sadness of Lent which imperceptibly is transformed into the joy of Easter, the summer and sun filled feasts of Ascension and Pentecost, August's profound pre-autumn celebration of Transfiguration and Dormition: are all these fiction? Delusion? Myth? Let's keep for a moment and concede that they are. But if so, why not at least make an attempt to understand what kind of deep approach to life undergirds these "myths"? For one fact is absolutely clear: the human element cannot live without holidays and feasts, without celebrations. Sociology, and not religious sociology by the way, long ago proved scientifically and objectively that fasts belong to the deepest, most primitive layer of life and culture. No society, no civilization has ever existed without feasts. Even anti-religious, militantly atheist society has its feasts and spawns its own cycle of celebrations: the Day of Work, the Day of Women, and so forth-one holiday after another. Even the festal rituals remain: processions, parades, flowers, singing, music, recreation, relaxation, parties, and banquets … we celebrate all kinds of events, but no matter what it is that gives rise to a particular celebration, what remains constant is the need for celebration.[1]

Schmemann points out a very important point regarding the human desire to celebrate life events. All cultures, nations, and societies have special celebrations, commemorations, and remembrances. In the United States we celebrate our freedom and liberty with parades and fireworks on the Fourth of July. Likewise, on Memorial Day we remember our departed soldiers and military personnel who died in order to protect our national freedoms. Throughout the year other important days are set aside to remember our "founding Fathers" on Presidents Day as well as the life and legacy of Martin Luther King, Jr. who fought for civil rights during the 1960's. We also celebrate our parents with Mother's Day in May and Father's

---

[1] Alexander Schmemann. *Celebration of Faith Volume 2: The Church Year*, (Crestwood, NY, St. Vladimir's Seminary Press, 1994), p. 14–15.

Day in June as well as Labor Day in September and Veteran's Day in November. All cultures commemorate the life cycle as birthdays, anniversaries, engagements, retirements, and graduations from high school and college.

Celebrating life events is not a modern phenomenon either. The ancient world was full of festal celebrations. The Romans celebrated the birthday of their great emperor, Augustus Caesar on September 23 by hosting speeches, parties, and festivities in his honor. Furthermore, the Old Testament is replete with various life cycle religious rituals such as Passover (Exodus 12), Sukkoth (Exodus 34), and the Feast of Trumpets/Rosh Hashannah (Leviticus 23). These festal celebrations included pilgrimages to the Jerusalem Temple as well as the eating of special foods and the singing songs which pertained to the feast day. The Gospels record that Jesus celebrated these feast days as well by eating the Passover meal with His disciples. After His death and resurrection the Book of Acts states that the disciples were celebrating the feast of Pentecost, a Jewish harvest festival when the Holy Spirit came upon them (Acts 2).

Many of the feast days such as Christmas have a long forty-day preparation period called Advent. The Advent season goes from November 15 until Christmas Day when we break the Advent fast with the Divine Liturgy. During Advent we participate in the sacraments of confession and communion, we hopefully engage in charitable work, and fast from certain types of food. Other feast days also have longer or shorter periods of preparation such as Pascha which has a long preparation period called Great Lent as well as the feast of the Dormition of the Theotokos which has a fifteen day fasting period from August 1 until August 15. Generally speaking the greater the feast, the longer the period of preparation. If you take some time to look at your Church calendar you will see these special Lenten or preparation periods highlighted in red.

F**IXED FEASTS AND MOVEABLE FEASTS**: Within the major feast days there are basically two types: fixed feasts and moveable feasts. The fixed feasts are those that are celebrated on a fixed day every year such as Jesus' birth on December 25 or His baptism in the Jordan on January 6. On the other hand, there are moveable feast days such as Palm Sunday, Ascension, and Pentecost which are celebrated depending on when Pascha is celebrated. Since the date of Pascha changes every year so do the days on which we celebrate the feasts associated with Pascha. Palm Sunday is always celebrated a week before Pascha, and likewise Ascension is celebrated forty days following Pascha and Pentecost fifty days after Pascha. Below are the feast days of the Church year organized into fixed and non-fixed:

Fixed Feasts

The Nativity of the Theotokos	(September 8)
The Exaltation of the Life-Creating Cross	(September 14)
The Entrance of the Theotokos into the Temple	(November 21)
The Nativity of our Lord Jesus Christ	(December 25)
The Epiphany of our Lord Jesus Christ	(January 6)
The Meeting of our Lord into the Temple	(February 2)
The Annunciation	(March 25)
The Transfiguration of our Lord Jesus Christ	(August 6)
The Dormition of the Theotokos	(August 15)

Moveable or Non-Fixed Feasts

The Entrance of our Lord Jesus Christ into Jerusalem
Pascha: The Lord's Resurrection
The Ascension of our Lord Jesus Christ
Pentecost: The Feast of the Holy Trinity

The majority of the festal celebrations are mentioned in Scripture, namely: Jesus' birth, the annunciation to Mary, and Jesus' entry into Jerusalem. Likewise, all feast days include beautiful prayers and hymns, but also contain many Scripture readings from both the Old and New Testaments. A full listing of the Scripture readings for the feast days are included in the back of this book for further reference.

However, not all feast day celebrations are included in the Bible. Feasts of Mary for example, her birth, and her entrance into the Temple, are recorded in the *Protoevangelion of James* which was written during the second century and was said to be authored by James the disciple of the Lord. During the first centuries of Christianity there were many gospels that were circulating throughout the Roman Empire. However, the Fathers of the Church gathered together in order to affirm which books should be contained in the Bible. This process did not happen quickly, but actually took centuries to decide which books to include in the canonical scriptures. The *Protoevangelion of James* was one of the gospels that was said to be authored by James the brother of the Lord and was written around the 2nd century. It was, however, not included in the Bible. The Gospel includes twenty-four short chapters that deal mostly about Mary and her role in Jesus' life; her birth, childhood in the Temple, and betrothal to Joseph who was said to be a widower who also had seven children from a previous wife. The Gospel also tells us that Jesus was born in a cave and that Zecheriah, the father of John the Baptist was martyred during the slaying of the Holy Innocents as reported in the Gospel of Matthew chapter 2.

Even though the Virgin Mary is mentioned infrequently in Scripture, Church Tradition drew upon the stories in the *Protoevangelion of James* for the background of these festal occasions. However, even though the background for the majority of Mary's feast days are from the *Protoevengelion of James*, each of the feast days in her honor is rich with Scripture readings from the Bible. Portions from the *Protoevangelion of James* are included in this book in order to show the reader the contextual background for the particular feast day for Mary as well as the actual Scripture readings that appear in the liturgical services themselves.

How To Use This Book: As with my previous books, *Feasts of Faith* was written for parish wide educational programs and is very practical for personal or group Bible studies. Many people like to prepare themselves for the liturgical services before coming to Church and *Feasts of Faith* could be used as a way to learn more about the Scripture readings that are associated with a particular feast. This book is not an exhaustive commentary on all of the Scripture readings for the feasts, but rather provides an overall introduction to the readings. The reader is encouraged to read all the Scripture references throughout the book in order to get a good appreciation of the message of God.

Many adult education classes devote an entire year for studying the feast days, taking one feast day at a time and reviewing the Scripture readings, liturgical hymnography, and studying the icon for the feast. This process is highly recommended because the Christian faith is expressed in both word and symbol. Taking time to review the may aspects of the festal celebrations are a good way to learn about Christian life and faith.

Before reading *Feasts of Faith*, take some quiet time away from the regular hustle and bustle of everyday life. This is not always easy because we are under constant barrage of emails, phone calls, faxes, not to mention the background noise of everyday living, television, radio, and the routine of home life. Find a quiet spot in your house such as a home office, back porch, or perhaps in a quiet place in a park.

Read through each chapter. Take time to look up the additional scripture references throughout the book. You also might want to take notes while you are reading too. While reading you might want to ask yourself: what is the message in this chapter? What is God saying to me and to the Church in these readings for the feast day? Does any particular word, phrase, image, or idea stand out in your mind? Are there key phrases or ideas that might be unfamiliar or strange to you? If you are using this book in a small group setting such as an adult education class you could use these questions as background material for your group discussion. I always find small group discussions very fruitful. These discussions generally lead to other questions of faith and allow other people to join in and share their thoughts and ideas. Finally it is always important to begin and end with prayer.

Feasts of Faith is a result of several years of pastoral work in parish ministry, especially with many newcomers to the Orthodox Faith. Through the course of many years I found that our Orthodox liturgical rites and rituals are rich with meaning. With every group of catechumens I go through the liturgical cycle of the Church, focusing primarily on the scriptural background and readings that form the basis for each festal celebration. Furthermore, the liturgical hymnography that we sing and hear are either directly or indirectly poetic reflections on scriptural texts and these too become the basis for teaching and learning. When we as a Church are continually reading and reflecting on Scripture, then the whole Church is being edified and encouraged. The more we read Scripture the more we learn about Jesus and his mission to the world and hopefully we will incarnate this mission in our lives, following him each and every day.

A final note regarding this book—the festal hymns and prayers encourage us to rejoice in God's salvation for today. Throughout the Church year we constantly come across the words "rejoice" or "joy": "Rejoice Mary full of grace the Lord is with you" or "Rejoice and be glad O Zion", or "through the cross joy has come into all the world." Nothing gives me greater joy than watching my two daughters, Hannah and Emma, grow and develop into young women. Watching them experience creation and the simple things of life, smelling flowers on a sunny morning, taking a dip in the lake, a walk in the woods, or baking brownies with daddy is a reason to take pause and rejoice in the great gift of children. When feeling discouraged or upset I take one look at their faces and my problems seem to disappear. This book is dedicated to Hannah and Emma and all children who remind us to rejoice in the small things in life!

CHAPTER ONE

THE NATIVITY OF THE MOST HOLY THEOTOKOS
(September 8)

Your Nativity, O Virgin, has proclaimed joy to the whole universe!
The Sun of Righteousness, Christ our God,
Has shone from you, O Theotokos!
By annulling the curse, He bestowed a blessing
By destroying death, He has granted us eternal life.

(*Troparion for the Feast of the Nativity of the Holy Theotokos*)

The first feast of the Church year that we encounter is the feast of the Nativity of the Most Holy Theotokos. The word "Nativity" simply means birth, so on this particular feast day we are celebrating Mary's birth and the events surrounding this birth. Mary's feast day is very special since it is also the first festal celebration of the Church year. If you look at your regular secular calendar the year begins on January 1. However, if you look at your Church calendar, you will see that it begins on September 1, which is also referred to as the "Indiction." The word "indiction" was an ancient way of making an announcement. The Roman's would often announce a war or a new tax levy by issuing an "indiction." Therefore September 1 is the announcement of a new Church year. At one point in time the new year began in March because it was associated with the springtime which was a time of fertility and when the farmers could begin working outdoors and plant their crops. Around the time of Jesus the New Year began on September 23 in honor of the Roman Emperor Augustus Caesar. It was under Augustus that there was a time of long-lasting peace, hence the term *Pax Romana*, Peace of the Romans. Then, sometime in the 6th century the New Year began on September 1. Since Mary's birth takes place on September 8, it is the first feast of the Church year.

Mary's birth is mentioned in the *Protoevangelion of James* in the following manner:

> And, behold, an angel of the Lord stood by, saying: Anna, Anna, the Lord has heard your prayer, and you shall conceive, and shall bring forth; and your seed shall be spoken of in all the world. And Anna said: As the Lord my God lives, if I beget either male or female, I will bring it as a gift to the Lord my God; and it shall minister to Him in holy things all the days of its life. (1 Samuel 1:11.) And, behold, two angels came, saying to her: Behold, Joachim your husband is coming with his flocks. For an angel of the Lord went down to him, saying: Joachim, Joachim, the Lord God has heard your prayer. Go down hence; for, behold, your wife Anna shall conceive. And Joachim went down and called his shepherds, saying: Bring me hither ten she-lambs without spot or blemish, and they shall be for the Lord my God; and bring me twelve tender calves, and they shall be for the priests and the elders; and a hundred goats for all the people. And, behold, Joachim came with his flocks; and Anna stood by the gate, and saw Joachim coming, and she ran and hung upon his neck, saying: Now I know that the Lord God has blessed me exceedingly; for, behold the widow no longer a widow, and I the childless shall conceive. And Joachim rested the first day in his house.

> And on the following day he brought his offerings, saying in himself: If the Lord God has been rendered gracious to me, the plate on the priest's forehead will make it manifest to me. And Joachim brought his offerings, and observed attentively the priest's plate when he went up to the altar of the Lord, and he saw no sin in himself. And Joachim said: Now I know that the Lord has been gracious unto me, and has remitted all my sins. And he went down from the temple of the Lord justified, and departed to his own house. And her months were fulfilled, and in the ninth month Anna brought forth. And she said to the midwife: What have I brought forth? and she said: A girl. And said Anna: My soul has been magnified this day. And she laid her down. And

the days having been fulfilled, Anna was purified, and gave the breast to the child, and called her name Mary.

These two passages mention Mary's parents as Joachim and Anna, who are also not mentioned in Scripture, but are commemorated at every liturgical service as the priest concludes the final dismissal by saying, "commemorating the righteous ancestors of God Joachim and Anna." Both Joachim and Anna are officially commemorated on the Church calendar on September 9, and Anna's death is commemorated on July 25. They are Mary's parents, and are depicted as a holy and righteous couple seeking God's salvation.

Mary's role in our salvation is deeply ingrained in the Church. She has inspired artists, sculptors, writers, and theologians. Hundreds of different types of icons have also been painted or written in her honor; probably the most popular being the Vladimir icon of the Mother of God as well as the icon entitled "Mother of the Sign," which depicts Mary with the Christ child in her womb and Mary's arm uplifted in prayer showing us that God used Mary's womb to bring about His saving work in the world. There are special prayer services called Akathists written in her honor as well as other liturgical hymns and hymnography.

In desperation the faithful have flocked to Mary for comfort and consolation. Songs and hymns have been dedicated in her honor and churches, seminaries, monasteries, and shrines have been erected in her memory. Mary's memory is very much alive for me because I am the rector of the Nativity of the Holy Virgin in Charlotte, NC. While driving through town I often come across other parishes dedicated in her honor such as The Queen of Peace, St. Mary's, or once while driving along a coastal town I came across the following name, "Our Lady of the Sea." Some of these names may seem odd to us yet they do reveal a deep love and devotion to the Mother of God.

Christians have also made pilgrimages to her shrines at Lourdes, Guadaloupe, and Chestehova and many in the East have venerated her icon in Kiev, Sitka, Smolensk, and Vladimir. Miracles have been ascribed to her intercessions and special services and prayers, such as Akathists, were written in her honor. The liturgical hymns and prayers refer to Mary as the Queen of Heaven, the Mediatrix, and most importantly the Theotokos, which is a Greek word meaning "the Mother of God" since she gave birth to the Son of God, Jesus Christ. The metaphors for Mary's role in salvation are rich and varied, they refer to her as the flower that bore the fruit, the golden censor, the New Jerusalem, the ewe that bore the lamb. Her womb is said to be more spacious than the heavens. Likewise, her name is invoked at every liturgical service as the deacon or priest prays, "Commemorating our most holy, most pure, most blessed and glorious Lady Theotokos and ever-virgin Mary with all the saints, let us commend ourselves and each other, and all our life unto Christ our God." The Divine Liturgy also includes a hymn to her after the consecration of the Eucharistic gifts of bread and wine as the choir sings, "It is truly meet to bless you O Theotokos, ever blessed and most pure and the mother of our God. More honorable than the Cherubim and more glorious beyond compare then the seraphim. Without defilement you gave birth to God the Word. True Theotokos we magnify you." During Great Lent this particular hymn is replaced by another one that begins, "All creation rejoices in you O full of grace ..."

Ironically, even though Mary's memory is highlighted in our liturgical prayer, she is only mentioned a few times by name in the New Testament. Sometimes she is referred to as the mother of Jesus without specifically referring to her proper name. In Cana of Galilee, at His mother's behest, Jesus performs His first public act by changing water into wine, "When the wine gave out, the mother of Jesus said to Him, "They have no wine." And Jesus said to her, "O woman, what have you to do with Me? My hour is not yet come." His mother said to the servants, "Do whatever He tells you" (John 2:3–5). Many people think that Jesus' speaks harshly to His mother here, yet the phrase "O woman" has nothing to do with being less of a mother. The meaning here is that Jesus was not yet ready for a public display of power as He says, "My hour has not yet come." His "hour" refers to His hour of glory which comes towards the end of His life on the cross. In the miracle at Cana, Jesus concedes and performs the miracle as we know that many believed in His name, "This was the first of His signs, Jesus did in Cana of Galilee, and manifested His glory; and His disciples believed in Him" (John 2:11).

In Luke 8:19–21 she is mentioned together with Jesus' family in the Gospel text which is read at many of her feast days, "Then His mother and His brothers came to Him, but they could not reach Him for the crowd. And He was told, 'Your mother and Your brothers are standing outside, desiring to see You.' But He said to them, 'My mother and My brothers are those who hear the word of God and do it.'" Jesus says that biological connection or lineage does amount too much since His "mother and brothers" are those who hear the word and keep it, a theme which is addressed throughout the Gospels.

Mary is also mentioned by John the Evangelist as one of the persons standing at the foot of the cross together with John the beloved disciple, "But standing by the cross of Jesus were His mother and His mother's sister, Mary the wife of Cleopas, and Mary Magdalene. When Jesus saw His mother, and the disciple whom he loved standing near, He said to His mother, 'Woman, behold your Son!' Then He said to the disciple, 'Behold your mother!' And from that hour the disciple took her to his own home" (John 19:25–27).

In the Book of Acts Mary is seen with the other disciples in the upper room at the feast of Pentecost when the Holy Spirit came upon the apostles in the form of fiery tongues (Acts 1:14). Likewise, in his epistles, the Apostle Paul makes only a passing mention of her in his epistle to the Galatians, "But when the time had fully come, God sent forth His Son, born of a woman, born under the law, to redeem those under the law, so that we may receive adoption as sons" (Galatians 4:4–7). Again, this does not mean that Paul has ill will towards Jesus' mother but that his emphasis in his epistles, particularly here in his letter to the Galatians, is that the messiah, who was promised to the house of Israel, has now come to fruition in a particular place and time in the birth of a woman. The fact that God chose Mary does not come through here in this passage but is an important one for both Matthew and Luke.

Despite the fact that Mary is not mentioned too often in the New Testament, she is remembered for her birth of our Lord. We remember her in prayer, sing praises to her in Church, venerate her icon in the services, and look to her for comfort and consolation.

The epistle reading for the feast of her birth is from Paul's letter to the Philippians. Philippi was a major Roman city located in northern Greece near Macedonia that was dedicated in honor of Philip of Macedon, the father of Alexander the Great, the one who fought Attila the Hun and united the Greek city-states. Philippi was a unique city because it was populated by retired Roman soldiers, which also meant that it was a predominately Gentile city, an area of non-Jews. It is most likely that Paul wrote this epistle from his prison in Ephesus as he alludes to this in the beginning of his letter, "I hold you in my heart, for you are all partakers with me of grace, both in my imprisonment and in the defense and confirmation of the Gospel" (Philippians 1:7). According to the book of Acts Paul seemed to have good connections with Philippi (Acts 16:11–15).

Paul begins his letter by encouraging their faith in Jesus, the faith that they received from Paul himself as well as encouraged by his fellow travelers and missionaries, "I thank my God in all my remembrance of you, always in every prayer of mine for you all making my prayer with joy, thankful for your partnership in the gospel from the first day until now" (Philippians 1:3–5). Then in the following chapter, Paul reminds the Philippians not to do anything from selfishness or from self-conceit but always out of respect for Christ. Paul encourages the Philippians, who have been newly received into the Church, to come together in a bond of love and solidarity with one another. In other words, only through following the Lord is one really being a disciple of Jesus. Paul stresses the humility of the cross as the pattern for discipleship, a theme that is echoed in the Gospel command, to take up ones cross and follow Him. This theme is also seen throughout Paul's letters since he envisions the cross as the central act of faith in Jesus. Paul offers the Philippians the following words:

> Have this mind among yourselves, which is yours in Christ Jesus, who, though He was in the form of God, did not count equality with God a thing to be grasped, but emptied Himself, taking the form of a servant, being born in the likeness of men. And being found in human form He humbled Himself and became obedient unto death, even death on a cross. Therefore God has highly exalted Him and bestowed on Him the name which is above every name, that at the name of Jesus every knee should bow, in heaven and on earth, and under the earth, and every tongue confess that Jesus Christ is Lord, to the glory of God the Father (Philippians 2:5–11).

Paul emphasizes the humility of Jesus, that Jesus became a servant of servants. In the Roman world a servant was more than just hired-help as we tend to think of maids and other cleaning professionals in our modern culture. During Jesus' time, servants were household slaves who were bought and sold in the marketplaces and were under complete obedience to their masters. The Gospel of Luke mentions that a Roman centurion, a high-ranking Roman official who was responsible for 100 men, begs Jesus to help him because his slave is at home and is sick, "For I am a man set under authority, with soldiers me, and I say to one, 'Go,' and he goes; and to another, 'Come,' and he comes and to my slave, 'Do this,' and he does it" (Luke 7:7–8. See also Matthew 8:5–13).

Very often slaves were captured during times of war and brought to the major cities where they were sold to wealthy landowners. There were many types of household slaves, some worked in the vineyards, others worked on farms, and others were in charge of educating their master's children. Some slaves were charged with cleaning visitor's feet as they entered the Roman household. Slaves were considered to the material and physical property of the owner.

Throughout his writings Paul often refers to himself as a servant or slave, "Paul and Timothy, servants of Christ Jesus" (Philippians

1:1). Also, we have a similar statement in the following verse from Romans:

> *Paul, a servant of Jesus Christ*, called to be an apostle, set apart for the Gospel of God, which He promised beforehand through the prophets in the holy Scriptures, the Gospel concerning his Son, who was descended from David according to the flesh and designated Son of God in power according to the Spirit of holiness by His resurrection from the dead, Jesus Christ our Lord, through whom we have received grace and apostleship to bring about the obedience of faith for the sake of His name among all the nations, including yourselves who are called to belong to Jesus Christ" (Romans 1:1–6).

> Am I now seeking the favor of men, or of God? Or am I trying to please men? If I were still trying to please men, *I should not be a servant of Christ* (Galatians 1:10).

> For what we preach is not ourselves, but Jesus Christ as Lord, *with ourselves as your servants,* for Jesus' sake (2 Corinthians 4:5).

The Gospels depict Jesus as the most perfect and humble servant, the one who devoted His life to other people. He had not earthly possessions of His own, He had no home or permanent residence. He told His disciples to only take with them the few things that were necessary for traveling, "Heal the sick, raise the dead, cleanse the lepers, cast out demons. You received without paying, give without pay. Take no gold, nor silver, or copper in your belts, no bag for your journey, nor two tunics nor sandals, nor staff; for the laborer deserves his food" (Matthew 10:8–10). Towards the end of His earthly ministry Jesus stoops down, takes off his tunic and clothes and washes the feet of His disciples, an image of real humility. He tells His disciples that they are to do the same for other people, just as I washed your feet, you go out and wash one another's feet, "For I have given you an example, that you should do as I have done to you, a servant is not greater than his master; nor is he who is sent greater than he who sent him. If you know these things, blessed are you that do them" (John 13:15–17). The mere thought of Jesus the Son of God, the one who performed miracles, walked on water, is the same one who also washed the feet of His disciples is extraordinary. Jesus' ministry of humility is an image for everyone, as He Himself reminds His disciples that the son of man came not to be served but to serve and give His life as a ransom for many.

Jesus' entire life and ministry was one of service. He served His disciples through His teachings as well as by example as He cleansed those possessed by demons and washed the feet of His disciples. Even though He had the power and authority over demons and nature He did not use His power as a force for oppression, but for love.

This theme of service is important since in Mary's own life was an act of humility and service. When the Angel Gabriel appeared to her and proclaimed the good news that she would bear Jesus, Mary responded affirmatively, "Let it be done according to your word." In other words, Mary accepted God's invitation and bore His son in the flesh, bringing about our salvation through her own womb. Later, when Mary visits her cousin Elizabeth who is also pregnant with a baby, John the Baptist, Mary says, "My soul magnifies the Lord, and my spirit rejoices in God my savior, for He has regarded the low estate of His handmaiden. For behold, henceforth all generations will call me blessed" (Luke 1:46–48). This prayer is also called the Magnificat the Latin word for "Magnify" and is nearly identical to Hannah's prayer in the Old Testament. After a time of infertility, Hannah finds herself pregnant with Samuel she dedicates him to the Temple as an offering of Thanksgiving (1 Samuel 2:1–10). Both Hannah and Mary are humble servants of the Lord, seeking to do His will in all things.

The hymns from the Nativity of Mary also echo the themes of humility and service. They are poetic reflections on the biblical story, that throughout the Scripture God works through human beings to bring about His salvation. Just as God worked through Abraham, Sarah, Moses, Joshua, Hannah, and the prophets, so too He worked through Mary:

> Today God who rests upon the spiritual thrones has made
> ready for Himself a holy throne upon the earth.

He who made firm the heavens in His wisdom has prepared a
living heaven in His love for man.
From a barren root He has made a life-giving branch spring up
      for us, even His Mother.
God of wonders and hope of the hopeless, glory be to Thee,
      O Lord.

Rejoice, O people
This is the day of the Lord
The palace of the light, the scroll of the word of life
Today comes forth from the womb
The gate facing the east is born
She awaits the entry of the great priest
She alone admits Christ into the universe
For the salvation of our souls

Today the barren gates are opened
The divine virgin prepares to enter
Today the fruit begins to blossom grace
Revealing the mother of God to the world
In her the earthly will unite with the heavenly
For the salvation of our souls

Today the barren Anna
Gives birth to the holy handmaiden of God
Who was chosen from all generations
For the fulfillment of the divine plan
To become the abode of the king
The creator of all, Christ our God
Therefore we mortals are restored
From corruption to eternal life.

(*Stikhera on "Lord I call," Great Vespers*)

These hymns echo the sentiment of humility which Paul highlights in his letter to the Philippians. The hymns speak about "the
fruit begins to blossom grace revealing the mother of God to the
world" and "who was chosen from all generations for the fulfillment
of the divine plan." Likewise, while the feast day is dedicated to Mary
and her birth, the hymns refer to her as secondary to Jesus, she is the

"palace of the light" and the "scroll of the word" as well as the "life giving branch." These references show that Mary is a container or conduit from whose womb contained the Son of God who is the light of the world and the Word of God. Mary is the palace of that light, the place from where the light shines as well as the material from which Jesus' is born, she being the scroll on which the Word of God takes shape and form. The hymnography for this feast as well as her other feasts are quite rich and expressive, reminding us of Mary's role in God's plan for salvation. Mary's birth allowed God to work through her in order to bring about the greater one who is Jesus. The Scripture and hymns for this particular feast, as well as all of her feasts, remind us that her role is always in function of her son's, that she is the one whom God has chosen to bring about our salvation and for that we are grateful.

CHAPTER TWO

THE EXALTATION OF
THE LIFE-CREATING CROSS
(SEPTEMBER 14)

O Lord, save Thy people
And bless Thine inheritance
Grant victories to the Orthodox Christians
Over their adversaries
And by virtue of Thy cross
Preserve Thy habitation

(*Troparion of the Exaltation of the Cross*)

The cross is a very important symbol in the Christian tradition and one cannot imagine being a Christian without it! The priest wears a pectoral cross as part of his liturgical vestments and uses a hand cross during the divine services. At the end of the Divine Liturgy we process to the front of the Church where we venerate a hand-cross that is held by the officiating priest. During baptism, the newly baptized child receives a cross as a part of his or her entrance into the Christian faith along with a long white baptismal garment. Likewise, a cross-bearer usually leads liturgical processions on feast days such as the Palm Sunday, Holy Friday, and for the Paschal vigil. A newly married couple takes their first walk together as a couple behind the officiating priest who holds a hand cross. Christians often wear a cross around their neck and hang a crucifix in their homes or offices as a reminder of their Christian faith. Most Churches have a cross on the cupolas or on their front door showing that this building is a special building — it is a Church! Sometimes the cross is such a common symbol that we even forget that it is right in front of us!

Twice a year we celebrate the cross in two special events. During the Third Week of Great Lent, which is also known as the Sunday of the Cross, we commemorate the cross by decorating it with flowers and placing it in the center of the Church. There are special hymns that are sung in honor of the cross and people prostrate themselves before the cross as well as venerate the cross as an act of faith. This reminds us that our Lenten journey is a journey to Golgotha as Jesus also accepts the cross as a part of His life ministry.

The other special occasion on which we commemorate the cross is on September 14 which is the feast of the Exaltation of the Life-Giving cross. This festal celebration is not found in Scripture but actually is a commemoration of an historical event: the finding of the true wood of the cross by Helen, the mother of Emperor Constantine. Constantine was the emperor of the Eastern Roman Empire and just before his victory over Maxentius in 312 AD he had a vision of the cross in the sky. Constantine also called the First Ecumenical Council in Nicea in 325 AD which brought together bishops from across the empire in order to discuss important theological and doctrinal topics, namely the person and work of Jesus Christ. The council at Nicea eventually formulated what is known as the Nicean-Creed, which later was amended at the Council of Constantinople in 381 AD, hence the name of our creed, the "Nicean-Constantinopolitan Creed." Constantine eventually accepted the Christian faith and therefore the eastern part of the Roman Empire adopted Christianity.

When Helen found the true cross, Patriarch Makarios of Jerusalem processed through Jerusalem with the cross of Christ and raising it so that everyone could see it and the crowds began to sing "Lord have mercy." This custom is still performed today by bishops and abbots of monasteries by taking the cross and blessing the four corners of the world with it: north, south, east, and west each time as the choir sings "Lord have mercy."

On the feast of the Exaltation of the Cross it is customary for a decorated cross to be placed in the middle of the Church while people approach and venerate it making prostrations and kissing the

cross. Many parishes also bless basil in honor of this feast day; basil in Greek means "king" and during the feast of the cross we are
celebrating Jesus who is our king. The liturgical hymns call to mind
particular events regarding the meaning and importance of the cross,
highlighting some prefiguring of the cross in the Old Testament as
well, mentioning especially the work of Moses stretching forth his
arms in the sign of the cross as he made the Red Sea part:

> The Cross is raised on high, and urges all creation to sing the
>   praises of the undefiled Passion of Him who was lifted upon it.
> From there it was that He killed our slayer,
> And brought the dead to life again;
> And in His exceeding goodness and compassion
> He made us beautiful and counted us worthy to be citizens of
>   heaven
> Therefore with rejoicing let us exalt His Name and magnify His
>   surpassing condescension.

> Moses prefigured thee, O precious Cross
> When he stretched out his hands on high and put Amalek the
>   tyrant to flight
> Thou art the boast of the faithful and succour of the persecuted
> The glory of the apostles the champion of the righteous
> And the preserver of the saints.
> Therefore beholding thee raised on high
> Creation rejoices and keeps feast
> Glorifying Christ who in His surpassing goodness through thee
>   has joined together that which was divided.

> O Venerable Cross, attended by the ranks of rejoicing angels
> Thou art exalted today
> Andy by divine command thou dost lift up again all those who
>   through the stealing of the fruit
> Had been made outcasts and were sunk in death.
> Therefore, embracing thee in faith with heart and lips from thee
> We draw sanctification and we cry aloud:
> Exalt ye Christ the God most good and venerate his footstool.

Come of people
Let us fall down in worship before the blessed tree
For by the cross, eternal justice has come to pass
The devil deceived Adam by the tree
Now, he has been deceived by the cross
He held the royal creation in bondage.
Now, he has been cast down an amazing fall
The serpents venom is washed by the blood of God
The curse is destroyed by the righteous sentence
Of the just one, who was condemned unjustly
The tree has been healed by the tree
The passion of the passionless God has destroyed
The passions of the condemned
Glory to thy dispensation, O Christ
Our gracious king and the lover of man

(*Stikhera on "Lord I call," Great Vespers*)

Even though the immediate context for the feast of the cross is based on historical facts, the finding of the cross by Constantine and Helen, the cross of course is a dominant theme throughout the Scriptures.

Several times in the New Testament we see that Jesus foretells the approaching end of His life. He knows that He will be going up to Jerusalem in order to be put on trial and to die. However, the Gospels record that His disciples did not want Jesus to do this, they wanted Him to be safe. Actually, when Peter, the chief disciple heard that Jesus was predicting His own demise, he rebuked Jesus in front of the other disciples. To rebuke someone is to verbally put them down with ones words, to castigate or berate them. Immediately after Jesus rebukes Peter, He takes His disciples aside and tells them, together with the crowds, that whoever would be His disciple must deny himself, take up his cross, and follow Jesus (Mark 8:34). This instruction is also mentioned in both Matthew 16:24–28 and in Luke 9:23–27, but in slightly different ways:

Then Jesus told His disciples, "If any man would come after Me, let him deny himself and take up his cross and follow Me. For whoever would save his life will lose it, and whoever loses his life for My sake will find it. For what will it profit a man, if he gains the whole world and forfeits his life?"

And He said to them all, "If any man would come after Me, let him deny himself, and take up his cross daily and follow Me. For whoever would save his life will lose it; and whoever loses his life for My sake, he will save it. For what does it profit a man if he gains the whole world and loses or forfeits his soul?"

Both readings are more or less identical, the main difference is that in Matthew Jesus directs His attention to the "disciples" while Luke tells us that Jesus directs His statement to "all" who were listening, both to the disciples and to the surrounding crowds. Furthermore, Luke also adds the word "daily" when Jesus says that His disciple must take up his cross "daily" which is a way of emphasizing every single day one must get up and take up the cross of Christ.

Taking up ones cross is also a very powerful statement because it is not only dying with Jesus but also requires suffering, self-denial, humility, and shame. When we see a crucifix, we might not always remember that crucifixion was a very shameful and public death. Crucifixion was a common method of capital punishment that was reserved for common criminals, thieves, and non-Roman citizens. A few details concerning the crucifixion process are needed in order for us to have a better picture of how the cross is considered shameful.

A criminal who was condemned for crucifixion had to carry a large piece of wood which served as the crossbar. The hands of the condemned person were attached to the wooden beam by a heavy rope. The tall upright portion of the cross remained fixed in the ground. Crucifixions took place outside of the city walls as a reminder to visitors not to break the law, they served as warnings or deterrents, very much like the "Don't Drink and Drive" signs that are on the side of the road. Many large cities had crosses lining the main road into the city gates as a public warning to obey the Roman law or they might wind up like the criminals hanging on the cross.

The condemned criminal was then beaten or as the Gospels say, "scourged" and then stripped naked, their hands were tied to the large horizontal piece of wood which was the crossbar. Their bodies were then lifted high upon the vertical piece of wood and they were left to hang there until they died. Crucifixion was also a very painful way to die since the person was going to die from asphyxia which is the lack of oxygen which took several hours. In the Gospels we know that Jesus hung on the cross for at least three hours if not more, "And when the sixth hour had come there was darkness over the whole land until the ninth hour" (Mark 15:33). The legs were sometimes broken in order to hasten death since the person's legs would be helping to hold up their bodies in order to get more oxygen. The Gospels mention that the Roman soldiers broke the legs of the two thieves who were crucified with Jesus but not His because when they came to break His legs Jesus was already dead, "So the soldiers came and broke the legs of the first, and of the other who had been crucified with Him, but when they came to Jesus and saw that He was already dead, they did not break His legs" (John 19:32). According to the Gospel of John Jesus is depicted as the Passover lamb who is slain for the sins of the world, echoing of course the Exodus story where the Lord tells Moses that the legs of the Passover lamb may not be broken, but rather, kept whole, "In one house shall it be eaten; you shall not carry forth any of the flesh outside the house, and you shall not break a bone of it. All the congregation of Israel shall keep it" (Exodus 12:46).

Crucifixion was certainly a shameful way to die. It was public, violent, and humiliating. Yet Jesus tells His disciples that taking up ones cross is a sign of discipleship. We are constantly reminded of this theme. Every time we make the sign of the cross over our bodies when we say our daily prayers we are reminded of our discipleship. When the priest blesses us with the sign of the cross we are reminded of our discipleship. When we encounter the feast of the cross we are reminded of our discipleship. When we hear the word cross we should think of the word "discipleship."

Perhaps the cross is such a prominent part of our life that we have forgotten its symbolic power. However, the Apostle Paul reminds us that the cross is truly powerful, "For the word of the cross is folly to those who are perishing, but to us who are being saved it is the power of God" and later on in the same passage Paul continues, "For Jews demand signs and Greeks see wisdom, but we preach Christ crucified, a stumbling block to Jews and folly to Gentiles, but to those who are called both Jews and Greeks Christ the power of God and the wisdom of God" (1 Corinthians 1:11 and 1:22–25). Jesus' death on the cross seemed to be a sign of weakness to the onlookers, who were shouting and deriding Him from below. They saw Jesus cure illnesses, drive out demons, and walk on water, but they saw His death as a sign of humiliation. Yet, Paul reminds us that the cross is powerful in that Jesus became totally empty of His own human power and strength and laid down His life for the sake of the world.

Paul reminds us that God raised and exalted Jesus Christ but He could only do so if Christ was completely obedient to Him. Again, Jesus is seen as the suffering servant, the one who bears the afflictions and pain of humanity in order to return us to God the Father. Jesus' death on the cross brings unity to the universe, as He Himself says in the Gospel of John, "When you have lifted up the Son of man, then you will know that I am He, and that I can do nothing on My own authority but speak thus as the Father taught Me. And He who sent Me is with Me; He has not left Me alone, for I always do what is pleasing to Him (John 8:27–30).

The Old Testament readings which are read during the Vigil or Great Vesper service the evening before which are from Exodus 15:22–16:1; Proverbs 3:11–18; and Isaiah 60: 11–16 which serve as background material for this feast. The reading from Exodus tells us the time when Moses led the Israelites through the Red Sea in order to escape Pharaoh's armies and chariots. The Israelites served the Egyptians in slavery working hard and building Pharaoh's temples. However, the Lord sent Moses as their leader, showing them the way to the Promised Land. After separating the waters of the Red Sea, the

Lord led the Israelites through safely getting them to the other side, as Miriam, the sister of Aaron sang, "Sing to the Lord, for He has triumphed gloriously; the horse and rider He has thrown into the sea" (Exodus 15:21). Exodus tells us that Moses led the Israelites for three days into the wilderness of Shur. Ironically, even though they were safe, three days into the wilderness the Israelites began to complain against the Lord. This will not be the first time that they complain. They complained because they were thirsty, the waters at Marah were bitter and the wilderness was a vast dry area. Moses then inquired of the Lord what to do, the Lord then showed Moses a tree and Moses through the tree into the water and the water became sweet. However, this is not the end of the story, the Lord also required something of the Israelites. He told them that He is giving them a promise that they must keep His statutes and ordinances which are laws. In other words, the Lord demanded that the Israelites obey His Word, a theme that is woven throughout the Bible. This image of a tree is important because it points forward to the tree of the cross whose memory is kept on this feast. The reading from Proverbs also highlights this theme as the author of Proverbs likens wisdom to a tree:

> Happy is the man who finds wisdom, and the man who gets understanding, for the gain from it is better than gain from silver and its profit better than gold. She is more precious than jewels, and nothing you can desire can compare with her. Long life is her right hand; in her left are riches and honor. Her ways are ways of pleasantness and all her paths are peace. She is a tree of life to those who lay hold of her; those who hold her fast are called happy (Proverbs 3:13–18).

Again, we see this theme of a tree compared with the teachings of the Lord. In both the book of Proverbs and the Psalms the stress is on keeping the Word of God, which is identical to the Law, ordinances, statutes, precepts, or commandments.

The readings from both Paul and the Gospel further highlight the importance of this feast. The Apostle Paul remind us that the cross is truly powerful:

"For the word of the cross is folly to those who are perishing, but to us who are being saved it is the power of God. For it is written, 'I will destroy the wisdom of the wise and the cleverness of the clever I will thwart.' Where is the wise man? Where is the scribe? Where is the debater of this age? Has not God made foolish the wisdom of the world? For since, in the wisdom of God, the world did not know God through wisdom, it pleased God through the folly of what we preach to save those who believe. For Jews demand signs and Greek seek wisdom, but we preach Christ crucified, a stumbling block to Jews and folly to Gentiles, but to those who are called, both Jews and Greeks, Christ the power of God and the wisdom of God. For the foolishness of God is wiser than men, and the weakness of God is stronger than men. For consider your call, brethren; not many of you were wise according to worldly standards, not many were powerful, not many were of noble birth; but God chose what is foolish in the world to shame the wise, God chose was is weak in the world to shame the strong. God chose, what is low and despised in the world, even things that are not, to bring to nothing things that are" (1 Corinthians 1:18–28).

According to Paul, Jesus' death on the cross seemed to be a sign of weakness to those who were watching, the crowds were shouting and deriding Him from afar. Throughout His life they saw Jesus cure illnesses, drive out demons, and walk on water, but they saw His death as a sign of humiliation and shame. Only criminals were crucified, not the Son of God. Jesus' death on the cross seems to go against human reason and understanding, after all, this seemingly powerful teacher named Jesus could not save Himself during His final hours. Surely ideas like these were also going through the minds of the Corinthians who were new to the faith. They were Gentile pagan's who accepted Paul's message of the Gospel, yet to them, the idea of a weak and powerless leader did not sound too good. Again, as Paul states in the first verse of the epistle reading, "For the word of the cross is folly to those who are perishing, but to us who are being saved it is the power of God" (1 Corinthians 18).

Paul reminds us that God raised and exalted Jesus Christ but He could only do so if Christ were completely obedient to Him. Again, Jesus is seen as the suffering servant, the one who bears the afflictions and pain of humanity in order to return us to God the Father. Jesus' death on the cross brings unity to the universe, as He Himself says in the Gospel of John, "When you have lifted up the Son of man, then you will know that I am He, and that I can do nothing on My own authority but speak thus as the Father taught Me. And He who sent Me is with Me; He has not left Me alone, for I always do what is pleasing to Him (John 8:27–30).

The repetition of Jesus' own end is intentional, it emphasizes that Jesus is identified with the suffering servant as we read in the writings of the prophet Isaiah:

> Surely he has borne our griefs and carried out sorrows; yet we esteemed him stricken, smitten by God and afflicted. But he was wounded for our transgressions, he was bruise for our iniquities; upon him was the chastisement that made us whole, and with his stripes we are healed. All we like sheep have gone astray; we have turned every one to his own way; and the Lord has laid on him the iniquity of us all. He was oppressed and afflicted, yet he opened not his mouth; like a lamb that is led to the slaughter, and like a sheep that before its shearers is dumb, so he opened not his mouth (Isaiah 53:4–7).

> The Lord God has given me the tongue of those who are taught, that I may know how to sustain with a word him that is weary. Morning by morning he wakens, he wakens my ear to hear those who are taught. The Lord God has opened my ear, and I was not rebellious, I turned not backward, I have my back to the smiters, and my cheeks to those who pulled on the beard; I hid not my face from shame and spitting (Isaiah 50:4–6).

> Behold, my servant shall prosper, he shall be exalted and lifted up, and shall be very high. As many were astonished at him, his appearance was so marred, beyond human semblance, and his form beyond that of the sons of men, so shall he startle many nations; kings shall shut their mouths because of him; for that

which has not been told them they shall see, and that which they have not heard they shall understand (Isaiah 52:13–15).

These passages from Isaiah are also read again during the services on Holy Friday during Holy Week. Jesus is identified with the suffering servant, the one who will be offered up as a blameless sacrifice on behalf of the sins of the people. Isaiah speaks about one who will bear afflictions, who is marred beyond resemblance, and by whose stripes we are healed. This sentiment is echoed in the Gospel of John as John reminds us that Jesus is the Lamb of God who takes away the sins of the world, a statement made by John the Baptist just prior to the beginning of Jesus' ministry (John 1:29–36). Towards the end of the Gospel, we see that Jesus is crucified outside of Jerusalem on the same day that the Passover lambs are being slain for the annual Passover supper. At Passover the Jews remembered God's saving hand in their lives. This image of salvation and sacrifice is enhanced in Jesus' own life as the Lamb of God who truly takes upon Himself the sins of the world.

The cross then is not merely a nice artistic addition to our Churches, but is really a constant reminder of our faith in the Lord. It was through the cross that Jesus trampled down death by His own death and through the cross that joy has come into the world. It seems strange that the cross is referred to in terms of joy, but it is the joy of the cross which Paul and the other apostles preached so boldly. In his letter to the Colossians, Paul states that the cross brings reconciliation and peace, "For in Him all the fullness of God was pleased to dwell, and through Him to reconcile to Himself all things, whether on earth or in heaven, making peace by the blood of his cross" (Colossians 1:20). This statement echoes the passage in the Gospel of John where Jesus says that when the son of man is lifted up he will draw all things to himself. Again, the cross brings about the unity of all, both Jew and Greek, male and female, we all stand before Him as equals before Him on Calvary.

CHAPTER THREE

THE ENTRANCE OF
THE THEOTOKOS INTO THE TEMPLE
(November 21)

Today is the prelude of the good will of God
The preaching of the salvation of mankind.
The Virgin appears in the Temple of God
In anticipation proclaiming Christ to all.
Let us rejoice and sing to her
Rejoice O Fulfillment of the Creator's dispensation

(*Troparion of the Entrance of the Theotokos into the Temple*)

Within Judaism there was a long-standing religious custom that parents dedicate their children to God by bringing them to the Temple in Jerusalem. At the feast of the Entrance of the Lord into the Temple on February 2 we celebrate Jesus' being brought to the Temple by His parents Joseph and Mary. The Old Testament offers us several examples of parents dedicating children to the Temple. The righteous Hannah promised the Lord that if she gave birth to a child she would dedicate her son to God. Hannah was the wife of the priest Elkanah and she was childless. After praying to the Lord, He gave her Samuel who later went onto to a great prophet in Israel, serving at the court of Saul and later defended David against Saul. Hannah's response to her birth-giving is to dedicate her son Samuel to the Temple. The Old Testament also states that upon the birth of a child the parents will dedicate them to the Lord by bringing them to the Temple and making a sacrificial offering:

> The Lord said to Moses, "Say to the people of Israel. If a woman conceives, and bears a male child, then she shall be unclean seven days, as at the time of her menstruation, she shall be unclean. And

on the eighth day the flesh of his foreskin shall be circumcised. Then she shall continue for thirty-three days in the blood of her purifying; she shall not touch any hallowed thing, nor come into the sanctuary, until the days of her purifying are completed. But if she bears a female child, then she shall be unclean two weeks, as in menstruation; and she shall continue in the blood of her purifying for sixty-six days. And when the days of her purifying are completed, whether for a son or for a daughter, she shall bring to the priest at the door of the tent of the meeting a lamb a year old for a burnt offering, and a young pigeon or a turtledove for a sin offering and he shall offer it before the Lord and make atonement for her, then she shall be clean from the flow of her blood. This is the law for her who bears a child, either male or female. And if she cannot afford a lamb, then she shall take two turtledoves or two young pigeons, one for a burnt offering and the other for a sin offering; and the priest shall make atonement for her, and she shall be clean (Leviticus 12:1–8. See also Exodus 13:2).

The text speaks of being "unclean" and in our modern mind this may seem absurd, after all, how can a woman who gave birth to a newborn child be "unclean" or "dirty"; giving birth is a beautiful act of love. There is nothing more beautiful than watching a child be born. However, we have to understand this against the common ancient understanding of purity and impurity. Blood is the "life force" in the body, without it we die! Since blood is needed to sustain life, the ancients considered blood to be holy or divine — from God Himself. Therefore, if blood is exposed to someone then that person is unclean. Throughout the book of Leviticus we see numerous examples of being clean and unclean. There usually are specific religious rituals that pertain to each type of "uncleaness." Being clean means to return back to the community as a full and active member. Therefore, that is why the idea of having a child would relegate a woman to be unclean and therefore have to make a sacrifice to God in order to be made clean again.

At the feast of the Entrance of the Theotokos into the Temple, we celebrate Mary being brought to the Temple by her parents Joachim and Anna as we see in the passage below:

And her months were added to the child. And the child was two years old, and Joachim said: Let us take her up to the temple of the Lord, that we may pay the vow that we have vowed, lest perchance the Lord send to us, and our offering be not received. And Anna said: Let us wait for the third year, in order that the child may not seek for father or mother. And Joachim said: So let us wait. And the child was three years old, and Joachim said: Invite the daughters of the Hebrews that are undefiled, and let them take each a lamp, and let them stand with the lamps burning, that the child may not turn back, and her heart be captivated from the temple of the Lord. And they did so until they went up into the temple of the Lord. And the priest received her, and kissed her, and blessed her, saying: The Lord has magnified your name in all generations. In you, on the last of the days, the Lord will manifest His redemption to the sons of Israel. And he set her down upon the third step of the altar, and the Lord God sent grace upon her; and she danced with her feet, and all the house of Israel loved her.

And her parents went down marvelling, and praising the Lord God, because the child had not turned back. And Mary was in the temple of the Lord as if she were a dove that dwelt there, and she received food from the hand of an angel. And when she was twelve years old there was held a council of the priests, saying: Behold, Mary has reached the age of twelve years in the temple of the Lord. What then shall we do with her, lest perchance she defile the sanctuary of the Lord? And they said to the high priest: Thou standest by the altar of the Lord; go in, and pray concerning her; and whatever the Lord shall manifest unto you, that also will we do. And the high priest went in, taking the robe with the twelve bells into the holy of holies; and he prayed concerning her.

Joachim and Anna brought their daughter to the Temple as an offering and there she stayed until she met Joseph who would later betroth her and take her to his own home. According to the *Protoevangelion of James* Mary was in the Temple serving the Lord and praying and offering thanks to God. In short, Mary was being prepared for her next step which would be to bear Jesus in her womb.

The epistle reading from Hebrews does not mention any of this information from the *Protoevangelion of James,* but it does refer quite a bit to the Jerusalem Temple and the rituals associated with it:

> Now even the first covenant had regulations for worship and an earthly sanctuary. For a tent was prepared, the outer one, in which were the lampstand and the table and the bread of the Presence; it is called the Holy Place. Behind the second curtain stood a tent called the Holy of Holies, having the golden altar of incense and the ark of the covenant covered on all sides with gold, which contained a golden urn holding the manna, and Aarons rod that budded, and the tables of the covenant; above it were the cherubim of glory overshadowing the mercy seat. Of these things we cannot now speak in detail. These preparations having thus been made, the priests go continually into the outer tent, performing their ritual duties; but into the second only the high priest goes, and he but once a year, and not without taking the blood which he offers for himself for the errors of the people (Hebrews 9:1–7).

The epistle to the Hebrews was written to a largely Jewish population which is seen in the numerous references to Israel or the rituals surrounding the Temple. It seems as if the entire letter is a description of religious worship but now seen in the context of the messiah Jesus and the new meaning that the Temple has for the believing Christian. There is no longer for the priestly tribe of Levi and Aaron who take care of the Temple worship since now we have the great High Priest Jesus Christ who offers the one perfect sacrifice on the cross for us. He is both our High Priest as well as the sacrifice itself, as John the Baptist calls Him the "lamb of God that takes away the sins of the world." The opening of the epistle to the Hebrews offers us greater insight into the overall message of the letter:

> In many and various ways God spoke of old to our fathers by the prophets; but in these last days he has spoken to us by a Son, whom He appointed heir of all things, through whom He also created the world. He reflects the glory of God and bears the very stamp of His nature, upholding the universe by His word

of power. When He had made purification for sins, He sat down at the right hand of the Majesty on high, having become much superior to angels as the name He has obtained is more excellent than theirs (Hebrews 1:1–4).

The opening of this letter shows us that while in the past the prophets spoke the Word of God to the Israelites, not only speaking about the messiah, but also calling them back to repentance and to serve the neighbor, God now has spoken to us by His Son, Jesus Christ, who is one greater than the prophets. Throughout the letter, the author goes to great length showing how their rites and rituals were only a shadow of the real hope which was perfectly revealed to us by Jesus.

Specifically in chapter 9, the author speaks about the Temple and the customs associated with it. He speaks about the lampstand and the table and the bread of the presence of which King David once ate, as well as the Ark of the Covenant and the altar of incense and Aaron's rod that budded:

> And you shall erect the tabernacle according to the plan for it which has been shown you on the mountain. "And you shall make a veil of blue and purple and scarlet stuff and fine twined linen; in skilled work shall it be made, with cherubim; and you shall hang it upon four pillars of acacia overlaid with gold, with hooks of gold, upon four bases of silver. And you shall hang the veil from the clasps, and bring the ark of the testimony in thither within the veil; and the veil shall separate for you the holy place from the most holy And you shall set the table outside the veil, and the lampstand on the south side of the tabernacle opposite the table; and you shall put the table on the north side. "And you shall make a screen for the door of the tent, of blue and purple and scarlet stuff and fine twined linen, embroidered with needlework. And you shall make for the screen five pillars of acacia, and overlay them with gold; their hooks shall be of gold, and you shall cast five bases of bronze for them (Exodus 26:30–37).

The Lord said to Moses, "Speak to the people of Israel, and get from them rods, one for each fathers' house, from all their leaders according to their fathers' houses, twelve rods. Write each man's name upon his rod, and write Aaron's name upon the rod of Levi. For there shall be one rod for the head of each fathers' house. Then you shall deposit them in the tent of meeting before the testimony, where I meet with you. And the rod of the man whom I choose shall sprout; thus I will make to cease from me the murmurings of the people of Israel, which they murmur against you." Moses spoke to the people of Israel; and all their leaders gave him rods, one for each leader, according to their fathers' houses, twelve rods; and the rod of Aaron was among their rods. And Moses deposited the rods before the Lord in the tent of the testimony. And on the morrow Moses went into the tent of the testimony; and behold, the rod of Aaron for the house of Levi had sprouted and put forth buds, and produced blossoms, and it bore ripe almonds. Then Moses brought out all the rods from before the Lord to all the people of Israel; and then looked, and each man took his rod. And the Lord said to Moses, "Put back the rod of Aaron before the testimony, to be kept as a sign for the rebels, that you may make an end of their murmurings against me, lest they die" (Numbers 17:1–10).

These were all part of the grand Temple worship which Israel enjoyed after their sojourn in the desert. The books of Leviticus and Numbers provide us with rich detail about the building of the Temple and its structured sacrificial system. However, the author of these books also reminds us that while the priests conducted the offerings of incense and the burnt offerings, it was the high priest who went into the Holy of Holies but once a year to offer prayers on behalf of all the people (Leviticus 16). The epistle to the Hebrews refers to Christ as our High Priest who will offer Himself as the most perfect and holy sacrifice which Hebrews speaks about throughout the letter.

This reading from Hebrews is read at the feast of Mary but actually speaks about Christ. Here we hear about the mercy seat, which is the seat of judgment, from which God will judge His people; the throne of judgment becomes the throne of mercy. However, the meaning of this passage from Hebrews is found a little later in the same chapter. Beginning with verse 11, Paul mentions that Christ is our high priest who enters into the Holy of Holies once and for all offering the perfect sacrifice, the sacrifice of His own blood which of course is accomplished for us through the cross:

> But when Christ appeared as a high priest of the good things that have come, then through the greater and more perfect tent (not made with hands, that is, not of this creation), He entered once for all into the Holy Place, taking not the blood of goats and calves but His own blood, thus securing an eternal redemption. For if the sprinkling of defiled persons with the blood of goats and bulls and with ashes of a heifer sanctifies for the purification of the flesh, how much more shall the blood of Christ, who through the eternal Spirit offered Himself without blemish to God, purify your conscience from dead works to serve the living God (Hebrews 9:11–14).

In other words Paul emphasizes the fact that Jesus is the true high priest who fulfills all priesthood, fulfilling the Levitical priesthood in the Old Testament. The Old Testament priesthood could not do what was needed, their repetitious sacrifices did not bring about true repentance as Hebrews says, only Christ could accomplish this great feat, "And every priest stands daily at His service, offering repeatedly the same sacrifices which can never take away sins. But when Christ had offered for all time a single sacrifice for sins, He sat down at the right hand of God, then to wait until His enemies should be made a stool for His feet (Hebrews 10:11–12). By fulfilling the priesthood He is fulfilling the entire Old Testament Law and ordinances which were set apart for the Israelites. Jesus then accomplished all things for us which is also mentioned earlier in the same letter to the Hebrews, "Since we have a great high priest who has passed through the heavens, Jesus, the Son of God, let us hold fast our confession. For we have not a high priest who is unable to sympathize with our weaknesses, but one who in every respect have been tempted as we are, yet without sin. Let us with confidence draw near to the throne of grace, that we may receive mercy and find grace to help in time of need (Hebrews 4:14–16). Christ is our High Priest who offered the one holy and pure sacrifice for us on the cross.

However, in order to become our great High Priest, the biblical God worked through His chosen vessel Mary, which the hymns refer to as the "Living Ark" and the "Tabernacle" which contained Jesus. We venerate Mary because she heard God's word and obeyed it, accepting to act according to God's will. During the feast of her entrance into the Temple the liturgical hymnography also plays on the Temple metaphor, Mary is the Temple that contained the Ark. In the Old Testament the Ark was a large container which held the Ten Commandments given to Moses on Mount Sinai. However, in preparation of this the hymns speak about Mary as herself entering the Temple in Jerusalem in order to serve God there as a child until she was old enough to bear children. While the hymns of course take poetic license and draw from both the epistle to the Hebrews and to the *Protoevangelion of James* they speak richly about the primary message of this feast day:

> Today let us, the faithful, dance for joy
> Singing to the Lord with psalms and hymns
> Venerating His hallowed Tabernacle
> The Living Ark, that contained the Word who cannot be contained.
> For she, a young child in the flesh, is offered in wondrous fashion
>   to the Lord
> And with rejoicing Zecheriah the great High Priest receives her as
>   the dwelling place of God.
>
> Today the living Temple of the holy glory of Christ our God
> She who alone among women is pure and blessed
> Is offered in the temple of the Law
> That she may make her dwelling in the sanctuary
> Joachim and Ann rejoice with her in spirit
> And choirs of virgins sing to the Lord
> Chanting psalms and honoring His Mother
> Thou O Virgin Mother of God
> Art she whom the prophets proclaimed
> Thou art the glory of the apostles and the pride of the martyrs

The restoration of all who dwell on earth
For through thee we are reconciled to God
Therefore we honor thy coming into the temple of the Lord;
And saved by thine intercession
With the angle we all cry to thee:
Hail Most Holy.

Today let the heavens greatly rejoice
Let the clouds pour down gladness
For behold, the gate that looks toward the East
Born according to the promise from a fruitless and barren womb
Is dedicated to God as His dwelling
Is led today into the temple as an offering without blemish
Let David greatly rejoice and strike his harp:
"Virgins," said he, "Shall be brought to the King after her.
Her companions shall be brought to thee
Within the tabernacle of God, within his place of propitiation
She shall be brought up, to become the dwelling place
Of Him who was begotten of the Father without change before all ages
For the salvation of our souls.

(*Stikhera on "Lord I call," Great Vespers*)

This feast honoring Mary really points to Christ who fulfills the entire Old Testament, the Law and the Prophetic teachings. Christ is our High Priest, the one who makes the one complete and perfect sacrifice on the cross and who offers Himself for our salvation. Christ completes what the Old Testament priesthood could not do, provide the perfect sacrifice for the sins of the people. However, in order to bring about our salvation through Christ, God worked through Mary and her obedience which included her entrance into the Temple.

CHAPTER FOUR

THE NATIVITY OF OUR LORD AND GOD AND SAVIOR JESUS CHRIST
(DECEMBER 25)

> Thy Nativity O Christ our God
> Has shown to the world the light of wisdom!
> For by it those who worshipped the stars
> Were taught by a star to adore thee the Sun of Righteousness
> And to know thee the Orient from on high
> O Lord glory to Thee
>
> (*Troparion of the Nativity of our Lord*)

According to the Orthodox Church calendar, the official name for Christmas is "The Nativity According to the Flesh of Our Lord God and Savior Jesus Christ," or sometimes referred to as simply the Nativity of our Lord. The Christmas season includes more than just the celebration on December 25, but also includes the Feast of the Circumcision and Naming of Jesus on January 1, the Baptism of Jesus in the Jordan River, which we also call Epiphany or Theophany, on January 6, and the Entrance of the Lord into the Temple on February 2. Together, these feasts are known as the "Winter Pascha," borrowing a term from the great Pascha in the spring when we celebrate the crucifixion and resurrection of Jesus Christ. These winter feasts celebrate three very important events in Jesus' life as He begins His preaching and teaching ministry in the world. At Christmas we celebrate the incarnation of the Word of God and is known to us as Jesus. We are celebrating the fulfilling of God's promise that He would send a messiah to save us from our sins.

The Christmas feast is preceded by a forty day period of preparation called Advent, which begins on November 15 and which lasts until the breaking of the fast with the Divine Liturgy on Christmas morning. Sometimes Advent is referred to as St. Philip's fast because it begins on the feast day of St. Philip, one of the twelve disciples. The word Advent comes from the French word "advenire," which means to come. In Advent then we are preparing for the coming of the Lord in the flesh. During the Advent season we are invited to participate in the sacrament of holy confession as well as increase our almsgiving to the poor and needy, especially in our local communities.

Advent does not begin with a special liturgical service as does Great Lent, there is no Rite of Forgiveness or special Lenten melodies which are used, but rather, we are gradually introduced into the preparation for the birth of Jesus. We hear the first mentioning of the coming birth of Christ on the eve of the Feast of the Entrance of the Theotokos into the Temple on November 21 where we hear the Christmas canon sung for the first time and we hear the phrase: *Christ is Born! Glorify Him!* which is sung during the weeks leading up to Christmas. Even at the end of November we are preparing ourselves to celebrate the Lord's birth. Advent is a season to take some time away from all the hustle and bustle surrounding us and to quietly reflect on the reason for the season which is of course the birth of Jesus. Sometimes we get so caught up in shopping, parties, and merrymaking that we can forget that at the very center of this celebration is the birth of the Son of God!

As we get closer to Christmas, we recall important persons of faith and events that lead up to the birth of Jesus. In early December we commemorate numerous prophets of the Church who preached the Word of God in difficult times, we especially remember Nahum (Dec. 1), Habbakuk (Dec. 2), and Zephanaih (Dec. 3). On the two Sunday's before Christmas, we remember the Holy Forefathers and Ancestors of God, the righteous men and women who prepared the way for Jesus. The Old Testament is full of stories about Abraham, Moses, David, Deborah, Judith, and Esther, as well as Joshua, Samson, Isaiah, and Ezekiel. These men and women remained faithful to God during wars, famine, plagues, exile, and in times of great poverty and oppression. Yet they are remembered for their commitment and dedication. Then, on the Sunday prior to Christmas we hear the gene-alogy of Jesus from the Gospel of Matthew. Again, we hear a long list of names and persons from Jesus' family lineage, both saints and sin-ners alike who came before Him preparing the way for our salvation (Matthew 1:1–18). Finally, five days prior to Christmas the Church serves the Pre-Feast services which are a combination of Vespers and Compline. The prayers, Scripture readings, and rich liturgical hym-nography reflect the beauty of the feast. We sing the troparion for the Prefeast which is a summary of our time before Christmas:

> Prepare O Bethlehem
> For Eden has been opened to all
> Adorn yourself O Ephratha
> For the Tree of Life blossoms forth from the Virgin in the cave
> Her womb is a spiritual paradise
> Planted with the fruit divine
> If eat of it we will live forever
> And not die like Adam
> Christ is coming to restore the image which He made in the beginning!

The Prefeast troparion prepares us for the Christmas celebration which we are eagerly awaiting. The Tree of Life is a scriptural reference to the Tree of Life in the garden of Eden. God told Adam and Eve that they could eat of anything in the garden. There were also two trees, the tree of Life and the tree of the knowledge of good and evil. God told Adam and Eve not to eat of the tree of the knowledge of good and evil, but they disobeyed His command. This hymn however refers to the tree of life which also appears in the book of Revelation, that this tree is given to us in the perfect gift of Mary's son Jesus. The "fruit" of her womb is Jesus who is our life-giver. Also, unlike Adam, if we eat of the tree of Life we will live forever with all the saints and not die like Adam did, disobeying God and being sent out of Paradise.

There are of course many aspects of the Christmas story, the shepherds keeping watch in the fields, the angelic message that Christ is born, and so forth. However, the Gospel reading for Christ-

mas focuses us about the visitation of the Magi or Wise Men to the
Christ child:

> Now when Jesus was born in Bethlehem of Judea in the days of
> Herod the king, behold, wise men from the East came to Jerusa-
> lem, saying, "Where is He who has been born king of the Jews?
> For we have seen His star in the East, and have come to worship
> Him. When Herod the king heard this, he was troubled, and
> all Jerusalem with him, and assembling all the chief priests and
> scribes of the people, he inquired of them where the Christ was
> to be born. They told him, "In Bethlehem of Judea, for so it is
> written by the prophet, 'and you, Bethlehem of Judea; are by no
> means least among the rulers of Judah; for from you shall come
> a ruler who will govern my people Israel ... When they saw the
> star, they rejoiced exceedingly with great joy; and going into the
> house they fell down and worshipped him. Then, opening their
> treasures, they offered him gifts, gold and frankincense and
> myrrh. And being warned in a dream not to return to Herod,
> they departed to their own country by another way'" (Matthew
> 2:1–3, 10–12).

Matthew ends this section of the chapter by telling us that these
wise men came bearing gifts of gold, frankincense, and myrhh. In the
medieval period the tradition developed that there were three wise
men whose names were Melchior, Casper, and Balthasar which later
became subjects for the Christmas song "We Three Kings," which is
sung at Christmas tableaus and plays during the Christmas season.
Matthew does not specify their names nor that there were three of
them, but only that wise men traveled from the east which echoes a
passage from Genesis:

> I see him, but not now; I behold him, but not nigh: a star shall
> come forth out of Jacob, and a scepter shall rise out of Israel; it
> shall crush the forehead of Moab, and break down all the sons
> of Sheth. Edome shall be dispossessed, Seir also, his enemies,
> shall be dispossessed, while Israel does valiantly. By Jacob shall
> dominion be exercised, and the survivors of cities be destroyed"
> (Genesis 24:17–19. See also Numbers 24:2–3, 5–9, 17–18).

We are not given too many details about these wise men, only that they came seeking to worship the baby Jesus and that when they saw the star in the East they rejoiced with exceedingly great joy (Matthew 2:10). The fact that they are from the "east" and that they are "wise men" tell us that they were sages or astrologers from a Gentile background. Thus, these wise men are from the Gentiles who were seeking out the Christ child.

Likewise, their gifts of gold, frankincense, and myrhh, are not just any type of gift, but point towards or foreshadow Jesus' death. Myrrh for example was used as an anointment to prepare corpses for burial and was used as a type of expensive perfume. The crucifixion narratives in Matthew, Mark, Luke, and John report that women came to the tomb very early on the first Easter morning in order to anoint Jesus' dead body, but He was not there because He was raised from the dead, "When the Sabbath was past, Mary Magdalene, and Mary the mother of James and Salome, bought spices, so that they might go an anoint Him" (Mark 16:1. See also Luke 24:1 and John 19:39). Likewise, both gold and frankincense were expensive products, gold represents wealth while frankincense was used for worship as we hear in one of the Psalms, "I call upon Thee, O Lord; make haste to me! Give ear to my voice, when I call to Thee! Let my prayer be counted as incense before Thee, and the lifting of my hands as an evening sacrifice!" (Psalm 141:2). Likewise, towards the end of the book of Isaiah, he mentions the appearance of all nations as affirming the strength of the Lord:

> Arise, shine, for your light has come, and the glory of the Lord has risen upon you. For behold darkness shall cover the earth, and thick darkness the peoples; but the Lord will arise upon you and his glory will be seen upon you. And nations shall come to your light, and kings to the brightness of your rising. Lift up your eyes round about, and see, they all gather together, they come to you; your sons shall come from far, and your daughters shall be carried in the arms. Then you shall see and be radiant, your heart shall thrill and rejoice; because the abundance of the

sea shall be turned to you, the wealth of nations shall come to you. A multitude of camels shall cover you, the young camels of Midian and Epaph; all those from Sheba shall come. They shall bring gold and frankincense, and shall proclaim the praise of the Lord. All the flocks of Kedar shall be gathered to you, the rams of Nebaioth shall minister to you; they come on my altar, and I will glorify my glorious house (Isaiah 60:1–7).

Earlier in the text, Isaiah prophesied concerning the utter destruction of God's people because of their great sin of idolatry, which both Amos and Hosea refer to as playing the harlot, Israel has run after other gods and thus has forsaken the God of Abraham, Isaac, and Jacob. Yet this biblical God is unlike other gods and is determined to remain faithful to His people, even if they continue playing games with Him, even idolatry. At the end of his book, Isaiah reminds his listeners that there is still hope for this people, that a light has arisen and will bring redemption to His people, "For I now their works and their thoughts, and I am coming to gather all nations and tongues; and they shall come and shall see my glory, and I will set a sign among them. And from them I will send survivors to the nations, to Tarshish, Put, and Lud, to draw the bow, to Tubal and Javan, to the coastlands afar off, that have not heard my fame or seen my glory; and they shall declare my glory among the nations" (Isaiah 66:18–23).

The visitation of the Magi is contrasted with that of the stubbornness and wickedness of King Herod. King Herod was referred to as King Herod the Great, the father of the Herodian dynasty and the father of Herod Antipas, the one who killed John the Baptist and who assisted Pontius Pilate in condemning Jesus to death (Luke 9:7 and 23:6–7). The Scriptures do not provide us with much information about Herod other that he was the King of the Jews or also referred to as the King of Judea. The Jewish historian Josephus tells us that Herod was an ambitious politician who was a very strong leader. He was alive during the death of Julius Caesar and befriended the famous Mark Antony. Later Herod was summoned to Rome where he received the title King of the Jews and returned back to Jerusalem as their King.

By the time Jesus was born, the Roman Empire controlled most of the known world around the Mediterranean Sea and was composed of various little kingdoms throughout the area. Herod was unpopular with many of the Jews since he was only part Jewish and he was also a foreigner. Although Matthew does not tell us directly, it is likely that any news about a newborn King would not be welcomed by Herod or his followers. After all, Herod was the king of Judea and had the full authority of the Roman government behind him, the mere mentioning of a newborn "king" would cause anxiety in most people, especially someone such as Herod.

After Herod inquired of the Magi where the Christ child was to be born he got into such a rage that he had all the male children who were two years old or younger killed so that they could kill the baby Jesus, which Matthew tells us is a fulfillment of a prophecy in Jeremiah, "A voice was heard in Ramah, wailing and loud lamentation, Rachel weeping for her children; she refused to be consoled, because they were no more" (Jeremiah 31:15). Herod was threatened by the new born Christ child. His response is quite expected since those in power and authority always seem to protect their power at all costs, even if it requires that someone else must be eliminated.

The Wise Men refer to Jesus as a king, a title that is referred to again and again throughout the New Testament. In the beginning of the Gospel of John Nathaniel says of Jesus, "Rabbi, You are the Son of God! You are the King of Israel!" (John 1:49). Later, in the same Gospel, Pontius Pilate, the Roman governor of Judea refers to Jesus as king, although not as a term of respect but a term of mocking:

> Pilate entered the praetorium again and called Jesus, and said to Him, "Are you the King of the Jews?" Jesus answered, "Do you say this on your own accord, or did others say it to you about Me?" Pilate answered, "Am I a Jew? Your own nation and the chief priests have handed You over to me; what have You done?" Jesus answered, "My kingship is not of this world; if My kingship were of this world, My servants would fight, that I may not be handed over to the Jews; but My kingship is not from this

world." Pilate said to Him, "So You are a king?" Jesus answered, "You say that I am a king. For this I was born, and for this I have come into the world, to bear witness to the truth. Everyone who is of the truth hears My voice." Pilate said to Him, "What is truth?" (John 18:33–38).

Throughout the Scriptures people affirm that Jesus is a king but Jesus never refers to Himself as a king, it is a title assigned to Him by other people. In his passion narrative Luke tells us that numerous persons from the crowd told Pilate that Jesus went around calling Himself a king and forbidding people to pay tribute to Caesar, an act of rebellion since all Roman citizens had to pay their share of taxes and honor Caesar as the Roman Emperor (Luke 23:1–5). Yet Jesus never stirred up a rebellion against the Romans nor did He forbid people to pay their taxes, actually the opposite is true. On one occasion He even told His disciples to render unto Caesar what is Caesar's and to Gods what is God's.

While Jesus never sought political authority and power, He spoke frequently about His Father's kingdom. He gave us numerous parables trying to teach His people what type of Kingdom this was, it was very different from what people had assumed. He used everyday images such as mustard seed, yeast mixed with flour, a camel going through an eye of a needle, and other images to show that God worked in ways unknown to man as the Prophet Isaiah says, "For my thoughts are not your thoughts, neither are your ways my ways" (Isaiah 55:8). At the end of His life it is quite ironic that this peaceful, loving, Jewish carpenter was sentenced to death for blasphemy and for treason, making Himself to be God and for rebelling against Rome. All four Gospels mention the fact that there was a sign on the cross which read Jesus King of the Jews, and the Gospel of John emphasizes that this was written in Greek, Latin, and Hebrew (John 19:20).

Herod's attempt at Jesus' life in the beginning of the Gospel functions as a foreshadowing of what is to come throughout the Gospel, since at nearly every step of the way there are those who are against Jesus and His ministry. Throughout the Scriptures the Pharisees,

Scribes, and Jewish leaders seek to put Jesus to death. Even Judas, one of His own disciples, betrays Him and His favorite disciple, Peter, denies Him three times! James and John, the sons of Zebedee, argue about who will be getting the best seats in the Kingdom and Nathaniel asks Philip if anything good comes from Nazareth. Thomas of course doubts that it was Jesus who was raised from the dead. Therefore, we should not be surprised when we read that evening at the beginning of His life Jesus was in danger. Every time He opened His mouth He was one more step closer to being arrested, stoned, misunderstood, and eventually betrayed. Yet we know that in the end God's victory prevailed in that He raised His Son Jesus Christ from the grave as a sign of His ultimate power and authority as the biblical God. Thankfully, this same promise of eternal life with Him is given to all of those who believe in the name of Jesus Christ and His Father.

The appearance of the wise men remind us that this birth is unlike other births, for the child who is born is going to be the savior of the world, "He will be great, and He will be called the Son of the Most High: and the Lord God will give to Him the throne of His father David, and He will reign over the house of Jacob forever; and of His kingdom there will be no end" (Luke 1:32–33):

> Let heaven and earth today make glad prophetically
> Angels and men let us keep the spiritual feast
> For God, born of a woman has appeared in the flesh to those who sit in darkness and shadow
> A cave and a manger have received Him.
> Shepherds announce the wonder; Magi from the east offer gifts in Bethlehem
> Let us, then, from our unworthy lips offer praise like the angels
> Glory to God in the highest and on earth peace
> For the expectation of the nations has come
> He has come and saved us from the bondage of the enemy.
>
> Heaven and earth are united today for Christ is born
> Today has God come upon earth and man gone to heaven
> Today for man's sake is seen in the flesh

He who by nature is invisible
Therefore let us also give glory and cry aloud to Him
Glory to God in the Highest and on earth peace
Which Thy coming has bestowed upon us O Savior glory to Thee.

Glory to God in the highest
I hear today in Bethlehem from the angels
Glory to Him whose good pleasure it was that there be peace on
earth
The Virgin is now more spacious than the heavens
Light has shone upon those in darkness and has exalted the lowly
who sing like the angels
Glory to God in the highest

Thou has come to dwell in a cave O Christ our God
And the manger received Thee: shepherds and Magi worshipped Thee.
Then was the preaching of the prophets fulfilled and the angelic
powers marveled
Crying aloud and saying:

Glory to Thy condescension of Thou who alone lovest mankind.

(*Litya Hymns at Compline for Nativity*)

CHAPTER FIVE

THE EPIPHANY OF OUR LORD AND GOD AND SAVIOR JESUS CHRIST

(JANUARY 6)

When Thou O Lord was baptized in the Jordan
The worship of the Trinity was made manifest
For the voice of the Father bare witness to Thee
And called Thee His beloved Son
And the Spirit in the form of a dove
Confirmed the truthfulness of His word
O Christ our God who hast revealed Thyself
And hast enlightened the world glory to Thee

(*Troparion for Epiphany*)

Most people think that the Christmas season is over on December 26. However, for Orthodox Christians we have a much longer celebration of the birth of Christ because we also extend the celebration of this feast with the celebration of both Jesus' baptism in the Jordan as well as His entrance into the Temple. These three feasts are wonderful opportunities for families to worship together because we are commemorating very important events in the life of our Lord, His birth, baptism, and entrance into the Temple. Epiphany and the Meeting of the Lord include special blessings as well, water and candles which are important educational opportunities for our children.

Jesus was baptized in the Jordan River. The Jordan is not really a wide river, it is quite small to other large ones, but it divides ancient Palestine lengthwise from east to west, starting at the Sea of Galilee and emptying into the Dead Sea. At some places it is only a few feet deep and at others it is very wide and deep.

Jesus' baptism in the Jordan River is called the "epiphany" or "theophany," which means "manifestation" since it is the manifestation of Jesus to the world as Jesus begins His public ministry. This event in the Gospels is celebrated on January 6 and includes the Great Blessing of Water. Baptism was a common cleansing ritual in the ancient world which symbolized not only renewal but also regeneration. The specific location of Jesus' baptism is very important because in the Old Testament it was the Jordan River which the Israelites had to cross in order to get over into the Promised Land and where the Prophet Elisha told Naaman that he wash and be cleansed:

> After the death of Moses the servant of the Lord, the Lord said to Joshua the son of Nun, Moses' minister, "Moses my servant is dead; now therefore arise, go over this Jordan, you and all this people, into the land which I am giving to them, to the people of Israel. Every place that the sole of your foot will tread upon I have given to you, as I promised to Moses. From the wilderness and this Lebanon as far as the great river, the river Euphrates, all the land of the Hittites to the Great Sea toward the going down of the sun shall be your territory. No man shall be able to stand before you all the days of your life, as I was with Moses so I will be with you; I will not fail or forsake you" (Joshua 1:1–2).

> "Behold, the ark of the covenant of the Lord of all the earth is to pass over before you into the Jordan. Now therefore, take twelve men from the tribes of Israel, from each tribe a man. And when the soles of the feet of the priest who bear the ark of the Lord, the Lord of all the earth, shall rest in the waters of the Jordan, the waters of the Jordan shall be stopped from flowing, and the waters coming down from above shall stand in one heap" (Joshua 3:11–13. See also Joshua 4:8–10 and Psalm 114:3–5).

> And Elisha sent a messenger to him, saying, "Go and wash in the Jordan seven times, and your flesh shall be restored, and you shall be clean." But Naaman was angry, and went away, saying, "Behold, I thought that he would surely come out to me, and stand, and call on the name of the Lord his God, and wave his hand over the place, and cure the leper. Are not Abana and

Pharpar, the rivers of Damascus, better than all the waters in Israel? Could I not wash in them, and be clean?" So he turned and went away in a rage. But his servants came near and said to him, "My father, if the prophet had commanded you to do some great thing, would you not have done it? How much rather, then, when he says to you, "Wash, and be clean? So he went down and dipped himself seven times in the Jordan, according to the word of the man of God; and his flesh was restored like the flesh of a little child, and he was clean" (2 Kings 5:10–14).

Baptism was not original with John the Baptist but goes back to the Old Testament times. The *mikvah* was a cleansing bathing ritual which the Jews performed as a way to ritually cleanse themselves. Jesus undergoes baptism to fulfill the Old Testament religious customs as we see in the following Old Testament passages. In the Scriptures, John is referred to as a "prophet" (Luke 7:26), "the baptist" (Matthew 3:1), the "the greatest born of women," (Luke 7:28), and the "voice crying in the wilderness (Mark 1:3). John is also known as the "forerunner" since he came before Jesus to prepare the way of repentance:

And this is the testimony of John, when the Jews sent priests and Levites from Jerusalem to ask him, "Who are you?" He confessed, he did not deny, but confessed, "I am not the Christ." And they asked him, "What then? Are you Elijah?" He said, "I am not." "Are you the prophet?" And he answered, "No." They said to him then, "Who are you? Let us have an answer for those who sent to us. What do you say about yourself?" He said, "I am the voice of one crying in the wilderness, 'Make straight the path of the Lord,' as the prophet Isaiah said." Now they had been sent from the Pharisee. They asked him, "Then why are you baptizing, if you are neither the Christ, nor Elijah, nor the prophet?" John answered them, "I baptize with water; but among you stands one whom you do not know, even he who comes after me, the thong of whose sandal I am not worthy to unite." This took place in Bethany beyond the Jordan, where John was baptizing (John 1:19–28).

John the baptizer appeared in the wilderness preaching a baptism of repentance for the forgiveness of sins. And there went

out to him all the country of Judea, and all the people of Jerusalem; and they were baptized by him in the river Jordan, confessing their sins (Mark 1:4–5. See also Matthew 3:1–12, Luke
3:1–20).

We know that Jesus was not baptized by John, because He needed
remission of sins, but so that His baptism would "fulfill all righteousness" (Matthew 3:15). However, while John was clearly baptizing and
preaching the gospel of repentance, some of John's followers thought
he himself was the Christ:

> And this is the testimony of John, when the Jews sent priests
> and Levites from Jerusalem to ask him, "Who are you?" He con-
> fessed, he did not deny, but confessed, "I am not the Christ."
> And they asked him, "What then? Are you Elijah?" He said, "I
> am not." Are you the prophet?" And he answered, "No." They
> said to him then, "Who are you? Let us have an answer for those
> who sent us. What do you say about yourself?" He said, "I am
> the voice of the one crying in the wilderness, "Make straight the
> way of the Lord," as the prophet Isaiah said (John 1:19–23).

John was a "voice of one crying in the desert." As a prophet, John
called people to repent and turn back to God. John's ministry reminding the Israelites to turn back to God and was preaching along
the same lines as Isaiah. Isaiah told the Israelites to stop worshipping
false gods and turn to the one true living God, the God of Abraham,
Isaac, and Jacob. However, the Israelites, like us, preferred to worship
false gods and idols, "Their land is filled with idols; they bow down to
the work of their hands, to what their own fingers have made" (Isaiah
2:8). John appeared as a voice in the wilderness, as another Isaiah, to
ultimately prepare the way for Jesus. However, John, like most of the
prophets, was persecuted for his preaching:

> At that time Herod the tetrarch heard about the fame of Je-
> sus; and he said to his servants, "This is John the Baptist, he
> has been raised from the dead; that is why these powers are
> at work in him." For Herod had seized John and bound him
> and put him in prison, for the sake of Herodias, his brother
> Philip's wife, because John said to him, "It is not lawful for you

to have her." And though he wanted to put him to death, he feared the people, because they held him to be a prophet. But when Herod's birthday came, the daughter of Herodias danced before the company, and pleased Herod, so that he promised an oath to give her whatever she might ask. Prompted by her mother, she said, "Give me the head of John the Baptist here on a platter." And the king was sorry; but because of his oaths and his guests he commanded it to be given; he sent and had John beheaded in the prison, and his head had was brought on a platter and given to the girl, and she brought it to her mother. And his disciples came, and took the body and buried it; and they went and told Jesus (Matthew 14:1–12).

Even in John's tragic death, he was a forerunner of the death of Jesus. Jesus called John the greatest born of women. This life of John the Baptist reminds us to hold fast to the message of repentance. John, along with the prophets and the early Christian witnesses, demonstrate that those who remain faithful will always be persecuted by the powers and principalities of this world.

We know from the Gospels that Jesus came to John to be baptized which recorded in all four Gospels (Matthew 3:1–16, Mark 1:9–11, Luke 3:21–22, and John 1:31–34). Matthew tells us that John was preaching in the wilderness of Judea and people were coming to him in order to be baptized. John appears to be hesitant at the fact that Jesus comes to him since Matthew says, "John would have prevented Him, saying, 'I need to be baptized by You, and do You come to me?'" (Matthew 3:14). However, Jesus consented to be baptized in order to fulfill all righteousness. At the end of the story Matthew tells us that there was a voice from heaven which said, "This is My beloved Son, with whom I am well pleased" (Matthew 3:17). Thus, Jesus' baptism is intimately connected with the word of God since it is the voice of God which announces this person Jesus as His Son.

This connection between baptism and preaching or baptism and the word of God is an important one because baptism is connected with the preaching of the Gospel. One of the final words from the risen Lord to His disciples was to continue preaching the Hospel and baptizing:

Now the eleven disciples went to Galilee to the mountain to which Jesus had directed them. And when they saw Him they worshipped Him; but some doubted. And Jesus came and said to them, "All authority in heaven and on earth has been given to Me. Go therefore and make disciples of all nations, baptizing them in the name of the Father, and of the Son and of the Holy Spirit, teaching them to observe all that I have commanded you; and lo, I am with you always, to the close of the age" (Matthew 28:16–20).

This preaching and teaching ministry is seen throughout the book of Acts well as through the witness of many sermons and theological orations from the Church Fathers. These catechetical orations were delivered to neophytes or catechumens who were learning about the way of Christ and were instructed in the Scriptures and doctrines of the Church before their baptism. Thus baptism was performed at the end of their instruction as a result of their repentance and acceptance of this new life in Christ. There was also post-baptismal instruction as well since the newly baptized were instructed in the basic tenants of the faith. Many of these sermons have been translated into English and can be purchased in book form or found online. These sermons are wonderful educational resources for review and reflection for individuals or groups.

A major part of the Epiphany service includes what is called the "Great Blessing of Water." This service includes additional Scripture readings as well as liturgical hymnography which speaks about the importance of Jesus' baptism. The priest recites a very long prayer which is very similar to the Offertory (Anaphora) prayer at the Divine Liturgy recalling God's greatness in creation; that the biblical God created the world out of the chaotic waters, that all of creation worships and sings His praises, that He promised us the great gift of salvation through the coming of the messiah, and so forth. In many ways this prayer is a summary of the Bible itself, recalling God's work in the world. At the end of the prayer the priest takes a handcross and places it in the water three times each time chanting the Epiphany troparion:

> When Thou O Lord was baptized in the Jordan
> The worship of the Trinity was made manifest
> For the voice of the Father bare witness to Thee
> And called Thee His beloved Son
> And the Spirit in the form of a dove
> Confirmed the truthfulness of His word
> O Christ our God who hast revealed Thyself
> And hast enlightened the world glory to Thee

Then the priest takes some of the blessed water and then blesses the Church with it, the altar, the icons, the sanctuary, and the people. During the month of January the priest will come and visit the parishioners' homes and bless their homes with this very same holy water.

Every year at Epiphany water is blessed not only to remember Jesus' baptism in the Jordan, but as a way to show that all of creation is included in God's love. The hymns for the water blessing are included below to further highlight the themes of this feast:

Hymns from the Blessing of Water:

The voice of the Lord upon the waters cries aloud saying:
Come ye all and receive the Spirit of wisdom the Spirit of understanding
The spirit of the fear of God
From Christ who is made manifest

Today the nature of the waters is sanctified
And the Jordan is parted in two
It holds back the stream of its own waters
Seeing the Master wash Himself

O Christ the King
Thou hast come unto the river as a man
And in Thy goodness Thou dost make haste to receive the baptism
Of a servant at the hands of the Forerunner
For the sake of our sins O Thou who lovest mankind.
At the voice of one crying in the wilderness

Prepare ye the way of the Lord
Thou hast come O Lord taking the form of a servant
And Thou who knowest not sin does ask for baptism
The waters saw thee and were afraid
The Forerunner was seized with trembling and cried aloud saying:
How shall the lamp illuminate the Light?
How shall the servant set his hand upon the Master?
O Savior who takest away the sin of the world, sanctify both men
and the waters.

CHAPTER SIX

THE MEETING OF OUR LORD JESUS CHRIST IN THE TEMPLE
(FEBRUARY 2)

Rejoice, O Virgin Theotokos
Full of grace
From you shone the sun of righteousness
Christ our God
Enlightening those who sat in darkness
Rejoice and be glad O righteous elder
You accepted in your arms the redeemer of our souls
Who grants us the resurrection

(*Troparion for the Meeting of the Lord into the Temple*)

Forty days after the Nativity of Jesus Christ we celebrate the feast of the Meeting of the Lord into the Temple on February 2. In addition to this feast it is usual for parishes to bless candles on this day.

The story behind this feast is recorded in the Gospel of Luke. According to the Law a woman had to offer a sacrifice in the temple for her purification forty days after childbirth. Mary and Joseph fulfilled the Law by bringing Jesus to the Temple along with two turtledoves. These were the sacrifices for those who could not attain a young lamb. At the Temple they were met by Simeon, who was "righteous and devout, looking for the consolation of Israel, and the Holy Spirit was upon him" (Luke 2:25). Simeon and Anna are only mentioned in Luke's Gospel, so we know nothing more about them other that what Luke tells us. Luke tells us that Anna was a prophetess and the daughter of Phanuel from the tribe of Asher. We do not know who Phanuel was, but the book of Joshua tells us that Asher was the fifth of the twelve tribes listed when the Israelites entered the offered a prayer to God. We recite or sing St. Simeon's Prayer at every Vesper Service:

> Lord, now lettest Thou Thy servant depart in peace,
> According to Thy word,
> For mine eyes have seen Thy salvation
> Which Thou has prepared in the presence of all peoples,
> A light for revelation to the Gentiles,
> And for the glory of Thy people Israel
> (Luke 2:29–32).

Simeon's prayer highlights God's salvation, light, and glory. These words are seen throughout the birth narratives. In the Gospel of Luke we hear that when the shepherds were in the fields watching their flocks they heard angels singing and praising God saying, "Glory to God in the highest, and on earth peace among men with whom He is well pleased!" (Luke 1:14). Likewise the star in the east which the Magi saw was the "light to the Gentiles" lighting the path for the Magi to come and worship the Christ child.

Simeon's prayer recalls the prophecies of Isaiah as he awaits the final salvation of God over the enemies of Israel. Isaiah reminds his readers that God redeems us. God sheds His light even on the Gentiles, and on the foreign nations, because all people are subject to Him:

> Thus says God, the Lord, who created the heavens and stretched them out, who spread forth the earth and what comes from it, who gives breath to the people upon it and spirit to those who walk in it; I am the Lord, I have called you in righteousness, I have taken you by the hand and kept you, I have given you as a covenant to the people, a light to the nations, to open the eyes that are blind to bring out the prisoners from the dungeon and from the prison those who sit in darkness. I am the Lord, that is my name; my glory I give to no other, nor my praise to graven images. Behold, the former things have come to pass, the new things I now declare, before thee spring forth, I tell you of them (Isaiah 42:6–9).

> How beautiful are the feet of him who brings good tidings, who publishes peace, who brings good tidings of good, who publishes salvation, who says to Zion, "Your God reigns." Hark your watch-

men lift up their voice, together they sing for joy; for eye to eye thee see the return of the Lord to Zion. Break forth together into singing you waste places of Jerusalem; for the Lord has comforted his people, he has redeemed Jerusalem. The Lord has bared his holy arm before the eyes of all the nations; and all the ends of the earth shall see the salvation of our God (Isaiah 52:7–10).

These two passages are found near the end of Isaiah. Earlier, Isaiah says that God finds no redemption in Israel, and predicts the utter destruction of God's people because of their injustice and unrighteousness. However, while Isaiah promises that God will eventually come to judge, He will also bring justice and equity among the peoples. There will be hope again and a new day will dawn, "As one whom his mother comforts, so I will comfort you; you shall be comforted in Jerusalem. You shall see and your heart shall rejoice; your bones shall flourish like the grass; and it shall be known that the hand of the Lord is with his servants, and his indignation is against his enemies" (Isaiah 66:13–16). In this new day includes the Gentiles or outsiders will also be welcomed into the house of God. His blessing will be extended to all nations.

In Luke' narrative, Simeon also addresses Jesus' mother Mary and foretells her son's future, "Behold, this child is set for the fall and rising of many in Israel, for a sign that is spoken against (and a sword will pierce through your own soul also), and thoughts out of many hearts will be revealed" (Luke 2:34–35). His words speak of Jesus' crucifixion and Mary's witness to this horrific event (John 19:25–27).

This scene in Luke ends with Anna giving thanks, "And coming up at that very hour she gave thanks to God, and spoke of Him to all who were looking for the redemption of Jerusalem" (Luke 2:38). Anna's words of thanks are important we get the word "eucharist." At the "eucharist" we are giving thanks to God for His Son Jesus and for the gift of salvation through the cross and resurrection. Joseph and Mary's offering of two turtledoves also symbolized thanksgiving as well as fulfillment of the Law. Likewise, Jesus' circumcision was also a form of thanks, and obedience to the Law.

The feast of the Meeting of the Lord is the culmination of the Christmas season. At the Meeting of the Lord Jesus enters the temple in Jerusalem where He is later found teaching and preaching the good news of the Kingdom:

> Now His parents went to Jerusalem every year at the feast of the Passover. And when He was twelve years old, they went up according to custom; and when the feast was ended, as they were returning, the boy Jesus stayed behind in Jerusalem. His parents did not know it, but supposing Him to be in the company they went a day's journey, and they sought Him among their kinsfolk and acquaintances; and when they did not find Him, they returned to Jerusalem, seeking Him. After three days they found Him in the temple, sitting among the teachers, listening to them and asking questions; and all who heard Him were amazed at His understanding and His answers. And when they saw Him they were astonished; and His mother said to Him, "Son, why have You treated us so? Behold, Your father and I have been looking for You anxiously." And He said to them, "How is it that you sought Me?" Did you not know that I must be in My Father's house?" And they did not understand the saying which He spoke to them. And He went down with them and came to Nazareth, and was obedient to them; and His mother kept these things in her heart. And Jesus increased in wisdom and in stature, and in favor with God and man (Luke 2:41–52).

The young Jesus astonishes His teachers with His learning, and throughout the Gospels, He continues to astonish the Pharisees and Sadducees in His teaching. They continually try to trap Him in His teaching but always seem to fail. Eventually they succeed in arresting Him and putting Him on trial, and finally to death. However, even at the end of His earthly life Jesus was obedient to His Father, eventually accepting the cross in order to save us. This obedience is seen throughout his life, during His childhood as well as an adult.

This Gospel reading however speaks about Jesus' teaching authority. Even at the young age of 12 years old, which was the common age of adulthood in ancient Israel, Jesus was teaching in the Temple.

It is hard to believe that such a young man was teaching wise elders in the synagogue, after all, men studied the Torah as well as the other books of the Bible before they began teaching. However, Luke tells us that this was Jesus' first public display of authority. Throughout the Gospels Jesus still seemed to shock the Jewish leaders and even His own disciples with His teaching:

> Simeon, tell us whom do you bear in your arms
> Why do you rejoice so greatly in the temple
> To whom do you cry and shout
> Now I am set free for I have seen my savior
> This is He who was born of a virgin
> This is He the Word, God of God
> This is He who for our sakes has taken flesh and saved men
> Let us worship Him
>
> Receive, O Simeon
> Him whom Moses once beheld darkness granting the law on Sinai
> He who has now become a babe subject to the law
> This is He who spoke through the law
> This is He whose voice was heard in the prophets
> This is He who for our sakes has taken flesh and saved men
> Let us worship Him
>
> Come and with divine songs let us also go to meet Christ
> Let us receive Him whose salvation Simeon saw
> This is He whom David announced
> This is He whose words spoke
> This is He who for our sakes has taken flesh and speaks to us in the law
> Let us worship Him
>
> Let the gate of heaven be opened today
> For He who is without beginning, the Word of the Father
> Has made a beginning in time without forsaking His divinity
> And as a babe forty days old
> He is of His own will brought by the Virgin, His mother
> As an offering in the temple of the law

The elder received Him in his arms crying as a servant to his Master
Let me depart for mine eyes have seen Thy salvation
Glory to Thee, O Lord, who has come into the world to save
mankind

(*Stikhera for "Lord I Call," Great Vespers*)

CHAPTER SEVEN

THE ANNUNCIATION TO THE MOST HOLY THEOTOKOS

(MARCH 25)

Today is the beginning of our salvation
The revelation of the eternal mystery
The Son of God becomes the Son of the Virgin
As Gabriel announces the coming of grace
Together with him let us cry to the Theotokos:
Rejoice, O Full of Grace, the Lord is with you

(*Troparion for the Annunciation*)

On March 25, nine months before Christmas, we celebrate the feast of the Annunciation. This feast commemorates the angel Gabriel bringing the good news to Mary that she will conceive and bear a son. This feast day is generally celebrated during the Lenten Fast and unlike the other feasts does not have a long post-festal period. It is one of those feast days and comes and goes very quickly, yet it is an important feast in the Church because it emphasizes the proclamation of the good news, the Gospel.

The Gospel reading for the Annunciation is taken from the first chapter of the Gospel of Luke which begins with the birth of John the Baptist. John's parents were Zacheriah who was a priest of the Lord, from the tribe of Levi and Elizabeth who was from a priestly lineage, a daughter of Aaron. In the Old Testament the Levitical priests were descendants of Aaron and sometimes we hear about the Aaronic priesthood (Luke 1:5–6). The angel Gabriel comes to Zacheriah telling him that his wife Elizabeth, who is advanced in years, will bear a son named John. After some time Elizabeth does give birth to John, and he eventually goes into the Judean wilderness preaching the gospel of repentance (Luke 3:1–17, Matthew 3:1–17; Mark 1:1–13).

After we encounter the birth of John, we come to the passage which retells the Annunciation of Gabriel to Mary. Angels are mentioned throughout the Scriptures and are known as God's messengers. In the book of Genesis an angel of the Lord wrestles with Jacob. After a long battle that lasted until the next morning, Jacob loses and his name is changed from Jacob to Israel (Genesis 28:10–17). An angel approaches the Prophet Isaiah and brings him a burning coal to touch his lips because he is a sinner (Isaiah 6:7). An angel comes to Joseph and reassures him not to divorce Mary but to care for her and her newborn child (Matthew 1:18–25). An angel appears to the myrhhbearing women as they approach the tomb on the first Easter Sunday and tells them to go tell the disciples that Jesus is risen from the dead. Likewise angels appear in the book of Revelation. The Old Testament mentions various types of angels, such as the cherubim and the seraphim. Likewise the Apostle Paul mentions the principalities and the powers. However, Gabriel is only mentioned twice by name in the Bible, once in the book of Daniel and then here in the Gospel of Luke:

> When I Daniel, had seen the vision, I sought to understand it; and behold, there stood before me one having the appearance of a man. And I heard a man's voice between the banks of the Ulali, and it called, "Gabriel, make this man understand the vision." So he came near where I stood; and when he came, I was frightened and fell upon my face. But he said to me, "Understand, O son of man, that the vision is for the time of the end" (Daniel 8:15–17).

> While I was speaking and praying confessing my sins and the sin of my people Israel, and presenting my supplication before the Lord my God for the holy hill of my God; while I was speaking in prayer, the man Gabriel, whom I had seen in the vision at the first, came to me in swift flight at the time of the evening sacrifice. He came and said to me, "O Daniel, I have now come out to give you wisdom and understanding. At the beginning of

your supplications a word went forth, and I have come to tell it to you, for you are greatly beloved; therefore consider the word and understand the vision" (Daniel 9:20–23).

In both passages from Daniel we notice that Gabriel came to Daniel in the appearance of a human person, as a man and therefore Daniel recognized him. Furthermore, Gabriel was sent to Daniel from God in order to interpret and explain the vision that Daniel had. The word angel means messenger and in the Scriptures the angels are messengers of God.

God sends the angel Gabriel to Mary in order to tell her the good news that she will bear a son. Luke records this encounter in the following way, "And he came to her and said, 'Hail, O favored one, the Lord is with you!' But she was greatly troubled at the saying, and considered in her mind what sort of greeting this might be. And the angel said to her, 'Do not be afraid, Mary, for you have found favor with God. And behold, you will conceive in your womb and bear a son, and you shall call his name Jesus'" (Luke 1:26–31). Luke continues by telling us that Mary accepted this invitation and pondered these words in her heart.

Throughout the Scriptures angels invoke fear in people. In his vision of the heavenly throne room, Isaiah vividly describes seraphim and cherubim flying around the heavenly throne singing, "Holy, holy, holy, is the Lord of hosts; the whole earth is full of his glory" (Isaiah 6:3). In his vision the earth is shaking and the temple is filled with smoke. Isaiah is not excited or happy to behold the glory of the Lord. Instead, he responds with fear, "Woe is me! For I am lost; for I am a man of unclean lips, and I dwell in the midst of a people of unclean lips, for my eyes have seen the King, the Lord of hosts" (Isaiah 6:5). People react in fear because they are encountering a messenger of God and the messenger is bringing the Gospel to them, the good news. In other words they are encountering the Word of God which is a fearful thing. When Moses approaches the burning bush on Mount Sinai, he has a sense of fear.

Gabriel tells Mary several important things in his message to her: that her son will be named Jesus, the Son of the Most High, He will inherit the throne of David, and that He will reign over the house of Jacob. These rather short verses tell us quite a bit of information. The name Jesus is the Greek form of the Hebrew name "Yeshua," which is the name Joshua. Joshua is mentioned in the Old Testament as a strong leader who leads the Israelites into the promised land. Moses dies just before entering so he designates Joshua to be the leader of the people:

> And Joshua the son of Nun was full of the spirit of wisdom for Moses had laid his hands upon him; so the people of Israel obeyed him, and did as the Lord had commanded Moses" (Deuteronomy 34:9–10).

> After the death of Moses the servant of the Lord, the Lord said to Joshua the son of Nun, Moses' minister, "Moses my servant is dead; now therefore arise, go over this Jordan, you and all this people, into the land which I am giving to them, to the people of Israel. Every place that the sole of your foot will tread upon I have given you to, as a promised to Moses. From the wilderness and this Lebanon as far as the great river, the river Euphrates, all the land of the Hittites to the Great Sea toward the going down of the sun shall be your territory (Joshua 1:1–5).

According to the Old Testament, Joshua is their savior because he brought them to the land flowing with milk and honey. The name Jesus is highly symbolic showing us that this child will be a savior as Joshua was a savior during the time of the Exodus.

Likewise, Gabriel says that Mary's son will be the son of the Most High. Throughout the Old Testament we notice that one of God's names is the Most High or the Almighty. These particular titles refer to strength, power, and authority. Another way of referring to power and authority, especially in terms of society and culture is to use political or legal terminology such as throne, judgment, or kingship. In the ancient world the king or emperor function as the father of all the people, they were the *pater familias*, the father of the family. The term for this very same concept was the patriarch, he was the father of the tribe or the clan, the chief of all the peoples. The patriarch or later the king not only led the nations in wars and battles but they also served to increase the wealth and power of the nation or area of land. The king was the last word in the ancient world. To speak of a throne then is to speak of kingly power and authority.

Gabriel also mentions that Mary's son will inherit the throne of David. David was a shepherd who was anointed by Samuel to be the new King and united both Israel to the north and Judah to the south. The Psalms are attributed to David, and he was the one who slew the giant Goliath. Furthermore, the Old Testament prophecies that we heard at Christmas time remind us that the messiah, the savior, was going to come from the throne or lineage of David. David was also mentioned of course in the genealogy of Jesus which we hear from in the gospel of Matthew, "The book of the genealogy of Jesus Christ, the son of David, the son of Abraham" (Matthew 1:1).

Gabriel's message might seem benign, every year during this feast we hear this Gospel and we see the iconographic image of the annunciation on many Christmas cards and in Churches. However, if we take this message in the context and background of the first century we realize its true power. We have to remember that during the birth of Jesus the Mediterranean world was under the power and authority of the Roman Empire which stretched from Rome up through England or what they called Britannia to the north, all the way across north Africa and into modern day Palestine and Turkey. This was a very large area and included different nations, languages, peoples and cultures.

Furthermore, it was during the reign of Augustus Caesar, who is also mentioned a little later in the Gospel of Luke, who was the first emperor to require public worship. In other words, Augustus Caesar demanded the people offer incense and thanksgiving before his statutes. We have evidence that one of his titles was also Augustus Caesar, "a son of a god." In previous generations, emperors were powerful and commanded respect and obedience, but with the reign of Augustus, we now have a stronger, much more potent attempt to align the emperor with the great mythological figures such as Zeus, Apollo, Aphrodite, and so forth.

Knowing this background gives us a better understanding of the annunciation to Mary. Luke is telling the world that even though Augustus Caesar rules the empire and that the Roman government and military is a strong force, it will be Mary's son Jesus who is the true king with the ultimate power and authority in the world. Ironically, in the passion narratives we know that Pontius Pilate himself requested that the title "Jesus, the King of the Jews" be placed on the cross, another annunciation to the world that indeed Jesus is the king. Of course this is ironic because Pontius Pilate is a Roman governor in Judea and in a way he is assisting the public proclamation of the Gospel by pointing out that Jesus is the king, not Caesar.

Mary's responds to Gabriel in the following manner, "How can this be, since I have no husband?" (Luke 1:34). Mary's question is very ordinary, after all, how can a virgin bear a child. However, Gabriel reminds Mary that with God all things are possible. If God made the heavens and the earth, parted the Red Sea to allow the Israelites to pass through, if He fed the Israelites the manna from heaven He can also allow the virgin birth! He is the God who is now working through Mary in order to bring a savior, a new Joshua:

> Revealing to you the pre-eternal Counsel
> Gabriel came and stood before you, O Maid
> And in greeting he said:
> Hail, O earth that has not been sown
> Hail O burning bush that remains unconsumed
> Hail, O Unsearchable Depth;
> Hail, O Bridge that leads to heaven;
> Hail, O Ladder raised on high that Jacob saw;
> Hail, O Divine Jar of manna;
> Hail, O Deliverance from the curse;
> Hail, O Restoration of Adam;
> The Lord is with you!
>
> You appeared to me in the form of a man
> Said the undefiled Man to the chief of the heavenly hosts
> How then do you speak to me of the things that pass man's power
> For you have said that God shall be with me,

And shall take up His dwelling in my womb
How shall I become the spacious habitation
And the holy place of Him that rides upon the cherubim?
Do not amuse me with deceit;
For I have not known pleasure,
I have not entered into wedlock
How then shall I bear a child?

Then the bodiless hosts replied
When God so wishes the order of nature is overcome,
And what is beyond man comes to pass.
Believe that my sayings are true,
O All-holy Lady
Entirely without spot
And she cried aloud:
Let it be unto me according to your word,
And I shall bear Him that is without flesh,
Who shall borrow flesh from me,
That through his mingling may He lead man up unto His ancient glory,
For He alone has power so to do.

Gabriel the archangel was sent from heaven
To announce to the Virgin the glad tidings of her conceiving;
And coming to Nazareth he pondered in amazement on this wonder.
O how shall He who dwells in the heights,
Whom none can comprehend, be born of a virgin?
How shall He whose throne is heaven and Whose footstool is the earth
Be held in the womb of a woman?
He upon Whom the six-winged seraphim and the many-eyed cherubim cannot gaze
He has been pleased at a single word to be made flesh of this His creature
It is the Word of God Who dwells within her
Why then do I stand here, and do not say to the maiden:
Rejoice, O Full of grace, the Lord is with you!
Rejoice, O Pure Virgin!

Rejoice, O Bride Unwedded!
Rejoice, O Mother of Life!
Blessed is the Fruit of your womb!

(*Stikhera on "Lord I call," Great Vespers*)

CHAPTER EIGHT

THE ENTRANCE OF OUR LORD JESUS CHRIST INTO JERUSALEM

By raising Lazarus from the dead before Thy passion
Thou didst confirm the universal resurrection O Christ God
Like the children with the palms of victory
We cry out to Thee: O vanguisher of death
Hosanna in the highest
Blessed is He that comes in the name of the Lord

(*Troparion of the Entrance of our Lord Jesus Christ into Jerusalem*)

One week before Jesus' resurrection we celebrate the feast of the Entrance of our Lord into Jerusalem, which is also referred to as Palm Sunday. On this day Christians throughout the world celebrate this special occasion in the life of our Lord by carrying palm branches and pussy willows in honor of our Jesus' triumphal entry into Jerusalem. Palm Sunday begins Holy Week the last week in the life of Jesus where we remember His betrayal, arrest, trial, and crucifixion.

However, the immediate context for Jesus' entry into Jerusalem is His raising of Lazarus from the dead. We are told that Lazarus was already dead for four days when his two sister's Mary and Martha were upset and came to Jesus begging Him to do something for their brother, "When Martha heard that Jesus was coming, she went and met Him, while Mary sat in the house. Martha said to Jesus, 'Lord, if You had been here, my brother would not have died. And even now I know that whatever You ask from God, God will give You.' Jesus said to her, 'Your brother will rise again.' Martha said to Him, 'I know that he will rise again in the resurrection at the last day.' Jesus said to her, 'I am the resurrection and the life he who believes in Me, though he die, yet shall he live'" (John 11:10–25). Martha seeks Jesus out because she knows that He has power. Throughout His ministry Jesus raises the dead, calms the storms, walks on water, and drives out demons. Upon meeting Mary and Martha, He tells them that He is the resurrection and the life and commands Lazarus to come out of his tomb:

> "Father, I thank Thee that Thou hast heard Me. I knew that Thou hearest me always, but I have said this on account of the people standing by, that they may believe that Thou didst send me." When He had said this, He cried out with a loud voice, "Lazarus come out." The dead man came out, his hands and his face wrapped in a cloth. Jesus said to him, "Unbind him and let him go" (John 11:41–44).

What makes the raising of Lazarus so powerful is that Lazarus was dead for four days. Being dead for four days is another way of saying that Lazarus was really dead and therefore the miracle is that much more powerful. John tells us that Lazarus came out of the tomb still with his burial clothes on, evidence that Lazarus was really and truly dead.

The next day we know that Jesus sends His disciples into Jerusalem in order to celebrate the Passover meal. The Passover was a special festal celebration in Judaism, and it commemorated the Israelites exodus out of Egypt. For centuries the Jews were in bondage and slavery to Pharaoh. God sent them Moses to lead them out of Egypt with a pillar of cloud by night and a pillar of fire by day. Every year the Lord commanded the Israelites to eat a special meal in commemoration of this salvific event. The Passover was not just an ordinary meal, but included memories of oppression and salvation, slavery, freedom, exile, and deliverance. Exodus chapter 12 tells us what the meal consisted: a young lamb, unleavened bread, and bitter herbs. Every year at the feast of Passover Jews remembered their bondage to Pharaoh and their subsequent deliverance out of Egypt. These strong memories were present at Jesus' last Passover.

Jerusalem would have been full of pilgrims coming to the city for the feast. The Passover was one of the biggest feast days on the Jewish calendar and there would have been many pilgrims coming from outlying areas in order to come and offer prayers in the Temple and partake of the Passover meal in Jerusalem, the holy city of the Jews. Coming to Jerusalem also meant spending a lot of money for food, lodging, and travel. If one traveled for one or two days journey they would need somewhere to stay as well as have food to eat.

Likewise, tensions during Passover would have been high. The regular presence of Roman guards and military were very strong. The Roman Prefect, Pontius Pilate was also in Jerusalem. He served as the governor of Judea from around 23–36 AD. Normally the governors lived in the Roman Gentile city called Caesarea, but due to the fact that Passover was a very important feast in the life of the Jewish people he needed to be in Jerusalem especially since at this time there were various small Jewish uprising throughout the area. One group of Jews, the Zealots, were against the Roman oppression of the Jews and wanted the area under Jewish not Roman rule. Overall political and social tensions were very high during the Passover feast. People would have been buying food stuffs as well as material goods for their travel. Lambs, herbs, and bread were the bases for the Passover meal, and of course wine.

The highly charged atmosphere of Passover was instilled in the rites and rituals surrounding the Passover feast. Passover festival commemorated the Israelites deliverance out of Egypt by Moses. When God told Moses that He was going to free the Israelites from slavery, He told Moses that they had to remember this great gift of salvation. Because they had to flee quickly they had to make unleavened bread and eat a very young lamb with herbs and other spices. They were to eat the Passover because it was a commemoration of God's defeat of Pharaoh, "Seven days you shall eat unleavened bread, and on the seventh day there shall be a feast to the Lord. Unleavened bread shall be eaten for seven days, no leavened bread shall be seen with you, and no leaven shall be seen in all your territory. And you shall tell your son on that day, 'It is because of what the Lord did for me when I came out of Egypt. And it shall be to you as a sign on your hand and as a memorial between your eyes, that the law of the Lord may be in your mouth; for with a strong hand the Lord has brought you out of Egypt'" (Exodus 13:6–8. See also Exodus 12, Leviticus 23:5, Deuteronomy 16:3–8, Numbers 28:16).

All of this information serves as the background for Palm Sunday, which is the beginning of the Passover week. Jesus was entering Jerusalem during the most important feast day of the Jews when tensions were high and when the city would have been filled with both Jews who were on pilgrimage as well as Roman military officials. The Gospel of John tells us that Jesus rides into the city on a donkey fulfilling the prophecy from Zecheriah, "Fear not, daughter of Zion; behold, your king is coming, sitting on an asses colt." This quotation in the Gospel of John is from two longer passages found in the Prophets Zecheriah and Zephaniah:

> Rejoice greatly, O daughter of Zion! Shout aloud, O daughter of Jerusalem! Lo, your king comes to you; triumphant and victorious as he, humble and riding on an ass, on a colt the foal of an ass. I will cut of the chariot from Ephraim and the war horse from Jerusalem; and the battle bow shall be cut off, and he shall command peace to the nations; his dominions shall be cut off form sea to sea, and from the River to the ends of the earth (Zecheriah 9:9–10).

> Sing aloud, O daughter of Zion; shout, O Israel! Rejoice and exult with all your heart, O daughter of Jerusalem. The Lord has taken away the judgments against you, he has cut out your enemies. The king of Israel, the Lord, is in your midst; you shall fear evil no more. On that day it shall be said to Jerusalem; Do not fear, O Zion: let not your hand grow weak. The Lord, your God, is in your midst, a warrior who gives victory; he will rejoice over you with gladness, he will renew you in his love; he will exult over you with loud singing as on a day of festival. I will remove disaster from you, so that you will not bear reproach for it. Behold, at that time I will deal with all your oppressors. I will save the lame and gather the outcast, and I will change their shame into praise and renown all the earth (Zephaniah 3:14–19).

Jesus fulfils these two prophecies as He humbly enters into the city on a donkey, a beast of burden. An earthly king would have entered with horses or on a chariot with a military procession showing his power and might. In our society a governor or president would enter the city in a long limousine procession with police cars and secret service. Television and media vans would probably follow. However, Jesus enters the city in a very quiet and humble manner, although the crowds want to make Him a king as they put out palm branches.

As Jesus enters Jerusalem the people cry out, "Hosanna, Blessed is He who comes in the name of the Lord, even the King of Israel" (John 11:13). The title "Hosanna" is the Hebrew word for "O save us." Furthermore, the phrase, "Blessed is He who comes in the name of the Lord" comes from Psalm 118:26, which is one of the Hallel Psalms which the Israelites recited and sang as they made procession up to the Temple in Jerusalem centuries before. "The Lord is God, and has given us light. Bring the festal procession with branches, up to the horns of the altar!" The Psalm recalls God's saving message of deliverance and hope, themes which of course are contained in this great feast day of the Church.

Ironically, the same crowd who greets Jesus in the city, giving Him praise, would later turn on Him when he was crucified. The crowd that exclaims "Hosanna," later exclaims, "Crucify Him! Crucify Him!" as the crowd wags their heads in disgust as their so-called king is crucified, "And Pilate again said to them, 'Then what shall I do with the man whom you call the King of the Jews?' And they cried out again, 'Crucify Him.' And Pilate said to them, 'Why, what evil has He done?' But they shouted all the more, 'Crucify Him.' So Pilate, wishing to satisfy the crowd, released for them Barabbas; and having scourged Jesus, he delivered Him to be crucified" (Mark 15:12–15). At first this reaction might seem strange, but it shows the wavering of humanity, that the crowds can be either for you or against you depending on their emotions. Throughout the Scriptures we see that the great crowds of people are certainly fickle, sometimes they want to make Jesus king and at

other times they want to stone Him. Luke records that right in the
beginning of Jesus' ministry they want to throw Him off the cliff
and kill Him. Other times the Jews want to gather and arrest Jesus
for making Himself to be like God.

The liturgical services for Jesus' entry into Jerusalem highlight
the events of both Lazarus Saturday and Palm Sunday. They reveal a
strong connection to the scriptural accounts as they are recorded and
presented to us in the Gospel of John, themes of salvation, freedom,
and hope:

> O new Israel, Church of the Gentiles
> Assemble today and sing with the Prophet Zecheriah
> Rejoice greatly, O daughter of Zion
> Shout for joy, O daughter of Jerusalem
> Behold, your king is coming to you
> He is meek, bearing salvation
> He rides on the colt of an ass
> Celebrate with the children, holding palms in your hands
> Hosanna in the highest
> Blessed is He that comes, the king of Israel

> By Thy command, O loving Lord
> Thou hast raised Lazarus Thy friend from death
> His flesh had been given over to corruption
> He was in the power of death four days
> By this, Thou has foretold Thy holy resurrection for us
> Today, Thou dost mount an untamed colt as Thy chariot
> Foretelling the conversion of the Gentiles
> Thy beloved Israel offers Thee a hymn of praise
> From the mouths of innocent children
> As they see Thee enter the Holy City, O Christ
> Six days before the feast of Passover

> Thou hast entered the Holy City, O Lord
> Riding on the colt of an ass
> Hastening to Thy passion
> That the law and the prophets might be fulfilled
> The Hebrew children greeted thee with palms and branches
> Heralding Thy victorious resurrection

Blessed art Thou, O savior
Have mercy on us.

Six days before the feast of Passover
Jesus came to Bethany
He restored Lazarus to life
Announcing the coming resurrection
Martha and Mary met Him, crying:
"Lord, if Thou hadst been here, our brother would not have died."
Jesus answered them
"Have I not already told you:
If anyone believes in Me,
Even if he dies, she shall live?
Show Me the place where you buried him."
Then the creator of all cried to him: "Lazarus, come forth."

(*Stikhera on "Lord I call," Great Vespers*)

Palm Sunday begins the Christian Holy Week services. During Holy Week we follow the last days of Jesus, His betrayal by Judas in the Garden of Gethsamane, His trial before Pontius Pilate and King Herod, as well as His scourging and beatings by the Roman soldiers, and then His crucifixion. The seemingly victory and power of Palm Sunday is quickly eclipsed by the darkness and sadness of Jesus' final days. However, the Scripture lessons for this feast also point us towards hope as well. That Jesus Christ is our King and Lord and that He frees us from our bondage to sin. The Christ child born quietly in Bethlehem is now publicly acknowledged as the King to the entire world. Both the Jews and the Romans come together to put Him on trial and to kill Him. Yet we look to the final hope which is firmly preached in His resurrection from the dead.

The feast of Palm Sunday and the many services for Holy Week contain many Scripture readings. You are encouraged to follow Jesus' final days by reading and praying the scriptural accounts of these last moments of his life. Holy Week can be a "mini-Lenten" journey and make Pascha even more meaningful for you and your family. The additional readings for Holy Week can be found at many online resources mentioned in the introduction or you can always ask your parish priest to help you locate these special readings.

CHAPTER NINE

PASCHA: THE RESURRECTION OF OUR LORD AND GOD AND SAVIOR JESUS CHRIST

Christ is risen from the dead
Trampling down death by death
And upon those in the tombs bestowing life!

(*Paschal Troparion*)

The Feast of the Resurrection, which is commonly referred to as "Pascha" is not one of the twelve feast days of the Church but is called the "Feast of Feasts" because of its importance in the life of faith. However, because Pascha is such an important feast day in the Church we have a lengthy preparatory period to get us ready for celebrating the death and resurrection of Jesus.

There are a series of five pre-Lenten or preparatory Sundays: the Sunday of Zachaeus, the Publican and the Pharisee, the Prodigal Son, the Last Judgment, and Forgiveness Sunday. On these particular Sundays we hear a series of Gospel readings that speak about repentance, forgiveness, prayer, and love. Likewise each Sunday has special liturgical hymns that prepare us for entering Lent emphasizing the importance of repentance.

On the last Sunday before Lent, called Forgiveness Sunday, it is a common tradition in many Orthodox Churches, that following the Divine Liturgy on this day the Church celebrates the Vespers of Forgiveness immediately followed by the Rite of Forgiveness. People ask one another for forgiveness before entering into the Lenten fast. During the solemn Vesper service we hear the following hymns which are poetic expositions on the previous gospel lessons which we heard during the preparatory Sundays:

The door of divine repentance has been opened
Let us enter with fervor having cleansed our bodies
Observing abstinence from foods and passions in obedience to
Christ
Who has called the whole world to His heavenly Kingdom
Offering to the Master of all this tithe of the year
That we may look with love upon His Holy Resurrection

The grace of the Lord has shone forth
The grace which illumines our souls
This is the acceptable time
The time of repentance is here
Let us put aside the works of darkness
Let us put on the armor of light
That passing though Lent as through a great sea
We may reach the third-day Resurrection of our Lord Jesus Christ
The savior of our souls

Let us begin the fast with joy
Let us give ourselves to spiritual efforts
Let us cleanse our souls
Let us cleanse our flesh
Let us fast from passions as we fast from foods
Taking pleasure in the good works of the Spirit
And accomplishing them in love
That we may be made worthy to the passion of Christ our God
And His Holy Pascha
Rejoicing with spiritual joy.

(*Stikhera for Forgiveness Sunday Vespers*)

Lent is not supposed to be a gloomy or drab time of year. Very often it can easily turn into a dark or morbid time, or even worse, a time for fulfilling mere obligations of fasting, prayer, confession, and Church attendance, following the rules and regulations of the Church, without a real change of heart. Lent is not about following rules or regulations, but about repentance, a change of heart. The Scriptures speak about having an open or softness of heart, a time where we are reminded of the supreme act of love. The book of Deuteronomy invites us to seek a heart of flesh rather than a heart of stone. A heart of flesh means that it is soft and pliable, ready for change. A heart of stone means that we have a hard heart unable to change and is not pliable. Seeking a soft heart and seeking a life of God also means that we will hopefully return to the Scriptures since the Word of God is the food which nourishes us and leads us back on the narrow path to the Kingdom. We turn to the Scriptures during Lent for guidance and direction hopefully returning back to them throughout the year.

Then, on the eve of Palm Sunday we enter into what is called Holy Week, a very special time in the year when Christians throughout the world commemorate the final days of Jesus' life, the last supper with His disciples, His prayer in the garden of Gethsamane, His arrest, trial, and crucifixion. Then on the night of Holy Saturday we begin our celebration of Pascha, the resurrection of our Lord. This feast is celebrated in a very special way. The Church is decorated from top to bottom with flowers and potted plants, the clergy wear white in honor of this special feast day and the choir sings a lot of special hymns that commemorate the different aspects of the death and resurrection of Jesus, the soldiers guarding the tomb, the myrhhbearing women, the angelic message of the resurrection. After a very long service that includes nocturns, matins, and the Divine Liturgy, the priest then blesses our Paschal baskets and we break the fast together as a parish family. During the next several weeks we will greet one another with the Paschal greeting, "Christ is Risen" and the response "Indeed He is Risen," which is often exchanged in different languages. Each parish may also have other local customs as well surrounding this wonderful feast.

During the Paschal Divine Liturgy of Saint John Chrysostom we begin reading from the Gospel of John:

> In the beginning was the Word, and the Word was with God, and the Word was God. He was in the beginning with God; all things were made through Him, and without Him was not anything made was made. In Him was life, and the life was the light of men. The light shines in the darkness and the darkness has

not overcome it. And there was a man sent from John. He came for testimony, to bear witness to the light, that all might believe through Him. He was not the light, but came to bear witness to the light. The true light that enlightens every man was coming into the world. He was in the world, and the world was made through Him, yet the world knew Him not. He came to His own home, and His own people received Him not. But to all who received Him, who believed in His name, He gave power to become children of God; who were born, not of blood nor of the will of the flesh nor of the will of man, but of God. And the word became flesh and dwelt (John 1:1–5).

The scriptural God is a God who speaks. According to the author of Genesis, God created through His word, "In the beginning God created the heavens and the earth. The earth was without form and void, and the darkness was upon the face of the deep, and the Spirit of God was moving over the face of the waters. And God said, 'Let there be light; and there was light'" (Genesis 1:1–3). He gave His word to Abraham promising that he will be the father of all nations, "No longer shall your name be Abram, but your name shall be Abraham; for I have you the father of a multitude of nations" (Genesis 17:5). He gave His word to Moses in the form of the Ten Commandments so that they would obey him, "And the Lord said to Moses, 'Thus you shall say to the people of Israel: 'You have seen for yourselves that I have talked with you from heaven'" (Exodus 20:21–22). He gave His word to Joshua promising him that he will lead the Israelites to Canaan, the land of milk and honey, "Moses My servant is dead; now therefore arise, go over this Jordan, you and all this people, into the land which I am giving to the people of Israel" (Joshua 1:2). He gave His word to the prophets in order to bring Israel back to repentance, "Wash yourselves; make yourselves clean; remove the evil of your doings from before My eyes" (Isaiah 1:16). He gave His word to the prophet Ezekiel and it was literally sweeter than honey:

And he said to me, "Son of man, eat what is offered to you; eat this scroll, and go, speak to the house of Israel." So I opened my mouth, and he gave me the scroll to eat. And he said to me, "Son of man, eat this scroll that I give you and fill your stomach with it." Then I ate it; and it was in my mouth as sweet as honey. And he said to me, "Son of man, go, get you to the house of Israel, and speak with my words to them. For you are not sent to a people of foreign speech and a hard language, but to the house of Israel — not to many peoples of foreign speech and a hard language, whose words you cannot understand. Surely, if I sent you to such, they would listen to you. But the house of Israel will not listen to you; for they are not willing to listen to me; because all the house of Israel are of a hard forehead and of a stubborn heart. Behold, I have made your face hard against their faces, and your forehead hard against their foreheads. Like adamant harder than flint have I made your forehead; fear them not, nor be dismayed at their looks, for they are a rebellious house." Moreover he said to me, "Son of man, all my words that I shall speak to you receive in your heart, and hear with your ears. And go, get you to the exiles, to your people, and say to them, `Thus says the Lord God'; whether they hear or refuse to hear." Then the Spirit lifted me up, and as the glory of the Lord arose from its place, I heard behind me the sound of a great earthquake; it was the sound of the wings of the living creatures as they touched one another, and the sound of the wheels beside them, that sounded like a great earthquake. The Spirit lifted me up and took me away, and I went in bitterness in the heat of my spirit, the hand of the Lord being strong upon me; and I came to the exiles at Tel-abib, who dwelt by the river Chebar. And I sat there overwhelmed among them seven days (Ezekiel 3:1–15).

God is fed up with the Israelites because they have turned their back on Him and have gone to worshipping other gods and idols. God gives Ezekiel a scroll to eat which is "sweeter than honey" as the text says and fills his stomach. His duty is to go and preach to the stiff-necked Israelites and call them back to repentance. Ezekiel is a very long book and the repetition of the phrase "stiff-necked" is encountered may times throughout the text, especially in chapter 32 and elsewhere.

Just as the biblical God spoke through His ten commandments on Mt. Sinai and as He spoke through the prophets so too He eventually spoke through His Son Jesus who is called the Word of Hod as we see in the opening sentences of the fourth Gospel, "In the beginning was the Word and the Word was with God and the Word was God" (John 1:1).

John presents his readers with more than mere words, but the ultimate Word, the Word made flesh. This Word is the way, the truth, and the life; the light of the world; the resurrection and the life; the Word which calls us to repentance, the Word which corrects and admonishes us, and the Word which is life-giving. At the end of John chapter 6 after Jesus multiplies the loaves and the fish and walks on water many people leave Him because His teaching is too strong. Jesus refers to Himself as the bread of life, the bread of heaven, and finally the living bread. At the end of the chapter as people leave Jesus he inquires of the twelve standing there, "Do you also wish to go away?" Simon Peter answered Him, "Lord, to whom shall we go? You have the words of eternal life; and we have believed, and have come to know that You are the Holy One of God" (John 6:67–69). Jesus gives life to us through His teaching which is the Gospel. The good news of salvation, that Jesus died and rose on the third day, which is what we are celebrating at Pascha, gives us life as we hear it preached in the Gospel and as we confirm this teaching when we receive the gifts of bread and wine, Jesus' body and blood in the Divine Liturgy. We are consuming the Word made flesh as we hear the Gospel and as we partake of the Eucharist. Each Divine Liturgy is really a little Pascha, a commemoration of the death and resurrection of Christ.

Beginning on Pascha and continuing for the next fifty days we will encounter the Word of God through the words of John the Theologian, so that we can all come to the knowledge of the one true living God who reveals Himself through Jesus Christ, the very Word of Life!

CHAPTER TEN

THE ASCENSION OF
OUR LORD SAVIOR JESUS CHRIST

Thou hast ascended in glory, O Christ our God
Granting joy to Thy disciples by the promise of the Holy Spirit
Through the blessing they were assured
That Thou art the Son of God, the Redeemer of the world.

(*Troparion Feast of Ascension of Our Lord Jesus Christ*)

The feast of Pascha is celebrated for a period of forty days. During this time we greet one another with the Paschal greeting: "Christ is Risen" and the response, "Indeed He is Risen." In addition, during this special time of the Church year you will also hear the Paschal hymns sung as we continue to proclaim the resurrection. Likewise, many priests travel to the local Orthodox cemetery and bless graves, which is often done on the first or second Sunday after Pascha. The Paschal celebration goes on for a long time.

On the fortieth day after Pascha we celebrate the Feast of the Ascension. Luke's Gospel tells us that after Jesus was raised from the dead He was found walking with His disciples on the road to Emmaus. Emmaus is only mentioned a few times in the Old Testament and is about seven miles northwest of Jerusalem. Two disciples are found walking to Emmaus, one named Cleopas and the other one is presumably Luke. Luke tells us that Jesus and broke bread with them (Luke 24:13–35). Luke continues by saying that Jesus appeared to His disciples and ate some broiled fish. Luke continues his narrative by telling us a very important understanding of Jesus' ministry and teaching:

Then He said to them, "These are My words which I spoke to
you while I was still with you, that everything written about Me
in the law of Moses and the prophets and in the Psalms must be
fulfilled." Then He opened their minds to understand the Scriptures, and He said to them, "Thus, it is written, that the Christ
should suffer and on the third day rise from the dead, and that
repentance and forgiveness of sins should be preached in His
name to all nations, beginning from Jerusalem. You are witnesses of these things" (Luke 24:44–48).

Luke tells us that, "Jesus opened their minds to understand the
Scriptures." This verse is very similar to the opening verses in John,
"No one has ever seen God; the only Son, who is in the bosom of
the Father, He has made Him known" (John 1:18). In other words
when we know Jesus, we come then can know His Father, "And this
is eternal life, that they know Thee the only true God, and Jesus
Christ whom Thou hast sent. I glorified Thee on earth, having accomplished the work which Thou gavest me to do; and now, Father,
glorify Thou me in Thy own presence with the glory which I had
with Thee before the world was made" (John 17:3–5). Jesus leads
us to God the Father so that we have eternal life with Him which
is seen throughout Jesus' preaching and teaching ministry. Jesus is
constantly teaching His disciples about doing the will of God. Jesus
provides access to the Father and thereby leading us to the heavenly
kingdom. Everything that Jesus said or did some how reflected the
will of His Father in heaven and that is why the Jews wanted to kill
Him. They thought that He was committing blasphemy by somehow
identifying Himself with God the Father.

Luke ends his Gospel with the following words, "Then He led
them out as far as Bethany, and lifting up His hands he blessed them.
While He blessed them He parted from them, and was carried up into
heaven. And they returned to Jerusalem with great joy, and were continually in the temple blessing God" (Luke 24:50–53). Bethany is about
two miles from Jerusalem and where Jesus stayed during the final week
before His death as is recorded in the Gospels (Matthew 21:17 and

Mark 11:1) and is also the place where Jesus' friends Lazarus whom He raised and his sisters Mary and Martha lived (John 11:1; 12:1).

However, in the first chapter of the book of Acts, which is also attributed to Luke, we encounter a somewhat different account of the same event:

> And when He had said this, as they were looking on He was lifted up, and a cloud took Him out of their sight. And while they were gazing into heaven as He went, behold, two men stood by them in white robes, and said, "Men of Galilee, why do you stand looking into heaven? This Jesus, who was taken up from you into heaven, will come in the same way as you saw Him go into heaven. Then they returned to Jerusalem from the mount called Olivet, which is near Jerusalem, a Sabbath days journey away (Acts 1:9–11).

Jesus' ascension into heaven takes place on a mountain called the Mount of Olives, the same location where Jesus prophecies the destruction of Jerusalem and the Temple, "and as He sat on the Mount of Olives opposite the temple, Peter and James and John and Andrew asked Him privately, 'Tell us, when will this be, and what will be the sign when these things are all to be accomplished?' and Jesus began to say to them, 'Take heed that no one leads you astray. Many will come in My name saying, 'I am He!' and they will lead many astray'" (Mark 13:3–5. See also Matthew 24:3, Luke 21:37, John 8:1). Jesus continues teaching His disciples about the rebellion of the nations and that because they follow Jesus that they will be arrested and condemned. This leads up to the final verses in Mark where Jesus warns His disciples about keeping "watchful" and "awake," because they do not know when the end will come but they should always be ready for it when it comes (Mark 13:32–37).

In Hebrew the term "Olives" or "Olivet" is related to the word for judgment which means that the Lord will come to the Mount of Olives as a judge and utter His divine justice and mercy. Both Zecheriah and Isaiah tells us what will take place:

> Thus says the Lord, behold, a day of the Lord is coming, on that day His feet shall stand on the Mount of Olives, which lies be-

fore Jerusalem on the east. On that day living waters shall flow out from Jerusalem, half of them to the eastern half and half of them to the western sea; it shall continue in summer as in winter. And the Lord will become king over all the earth; on that day the Lord will be one and His name one. The whole land shall be turned into a plain from Geba to Rimmon south of Jerusalem. But Jerusalem shall remain aloft upon its site from the Gate of Benjamin to the place of the former gate, to the Corner gate, and from the Tower of Hananel to the king's wine presses. And it shall be inhabited, for there shall be no more curse, Jerusalem shall dwell in security (Zecheriah 14:1, 4, 8–11).

It shall come to pass in the latter days that the mountain of the house of the Lord shall be established as the highest of the mountains, and shall be raised above the hills; and all nations shall flow to it, and many people shall come, and say: "Come, let us go up to the mountain of the Lord, to the house of the God of Jacob; that He may teach us His ways that we may walk in His paths. For our of Zion shall go forth the law, and the word of the Lord from Jerusalem. He shall judge between the nations, and shall decide for many peoples; and they shall beat their swords into plowshares, and their spears into pruning hooks; nation shall not lift up sword against nation, neither shall they learn war any more (Isaiah 2:2–4).

Jesus goes to Bethany to the Mount of Olives, the mountain of judgment as we recite every week in the Creed, "and he ascended into heaven and sits at the right hand of God the Father. And he shall come again to judge the living and the dead whose kingdom shall have no end." Jesus ascends to heaven in order to complete His mission and ministry and to sit at the right hand of God the Father. We also know that He will come again to judge the world and will come again just as He ascended, with the power and authority of God the Father. Jesus ascends to the Father in order to execute judgment of which Zecheriah and the other prophets spoke about. Jesus is the true judge and judges justly. Thankfully He is also the merciful God who does not hold our sins against us, otherwise we would not survive.

The earthly kings of Israel were supposed to mitigate justice for the people. When we read 1–2 Kings and 1–2 Chronicles we see that the earthly kings were corrupt and evil. They did not do what they were supposed to do. Only Jesus, as the Scriptures say, was the only righteous one. As the judge Jesus calls us to account for our life which is seen in several scriptural stories such as the Sheep and the Goats, the parables of the talents, as well as the parable of the vineyard. We are responsible for our life and for everything that with which God has entrusted us. Our judgment will be on the love of both God and neighbor. In other words we will be judged on love. The Scriptures, it seems, are very clear that loving God is intimately bound with loving the neighbor as we see in the first epistle of John, "For he who does not love his brother whom he has seen, cannot love God whom he has not seen" (1 John 4:20), which echoes of course earlier writings of the prophets, especially Amos for example, "Therefore, because you trample upon the poor and take from him exactions of wheat, you have built houses of hewn stone, but you shall not dwell in them; you have planted vineyards, but you shall not drink their wine" (Amos 5:10–11) and later, "Woe to those who lie upon beds of ivory, and stretch themselves upon their couches, and eat lambs from the flock, and calves from the midst of the harp, and like David invent for themselves instruments of music; who drink wine in bowls, and anoint themselves with the finest oils" (Amos 6:4–6). The love of the neighbor is highlighted in the liturgical prayers of the Church which specifically refer to Jesus as the *philanthropos* — "lover of mankind," which is mentioned at least six times during the Divine Liturgy. At the priestly prayer of the First Antiphon the priest exclaims, "O Lord our God, Thy power is incomparable. Thy power is incomprehensible. Thy mercy is immeasurable. *Thy love for mankind is inexpressible.* Look down on us and on this holy house with pity, O Master, and impart the riches of Thy mercy and Thy compassion to us and to those who pray with us."[1]

---

[1] Prayer of the First Antiphon Divine Liturgy of St. John Chrysostom (South Canaan, PA: St. Tikhon's Seminary Press, 1967), p. 31. See also the "litany before the Lord's Prayer", prayer of "thanksgiving", and the prayers of the two final

At the end of the long Anaphora (Offertory) prayer we are asked to call to mind those who are less fortunate than we are, the sick and the suffering, as well as the poor:

> Remember, O Lord, the city in which we dwell, every city and country, those who in faith dwell in them. Remember O Lord, travelers by land, by sea, and by air, the sick and the suffering; captives, and their salvation. Remember, O Lord, those who bring offerings and do good in thy holy Churches; *those who remember the poor; and upon us all send forth Thy mercies.*[2]

On the one hand the feast of Ascension is a wonderful event as we prepare to conclude the Paschal season. However, on the other hand it is a warning since Jesus ascends to be with His Father and will return as He ascended, in all power and glory. He will return again as the judge over all creation. Therefore, there is much work to be done. Between now and the second coming of Christ it is our job to literally be the hands and feet of Christ in the world, offering our prayers and hymns to God as well as feeding the poor, clothing the naked, and comforting the distressed. Ascension is a reminder of Jesus' command in the Gospel of John to wash each other's feet, an act of humility and service. Even though at the feast of Pentecost we receive the Holy Spirit which is a sign of the "end times," we anticipate this gift at Ascension. Jesus ascends to His heavenly Father in order to send the Spirit into the world. In many ways Jesus' memory is more powerful after His ascension than during His earthly life:

> The Lord ascended to heaven
> To send the comforter into the world

---

blessings which all refer to the Lord as the "lover of mankind."
[2] Divine Liturgy of St. John Chrysostom, p. 70. A similar but longer prayer is found in the Liturgy of St. Basil the Great. St. Basil's prayer is an extended version of the one that we find in St. John's liturgy and emphasizes the many types of people who are suffering throughout the world, "*and those who remember the poor; reward them with Thy rich and heavenly gifts; for their earthly temporal, and corruptible gifts, do though grant them heavenly ones, eternal and incorruptible. Remember O Lord, those who are in the deserts, mountains, caverns and pits of the earth... defend the widows, protect the orphans, free the captives; heal the sick.*"

The heavens prepared His throne the clouds His royal mount
The angels were amazed seeing a man exalted
The Father awaits His co-eternal son
The Holy Spirit command the angels
Lift up your hands O you gates
Clap your hands all you nations
For Christ has ascended to where He was before

The cherubim were amazed at thine ascension
They beheld the God of angels ascending the clouds
We glorify Thee for Thy mercy is good
O Lord glory to Thee

Seeing Thine ascension O giver of life
The apostles mourned and wept
Master do not leave us Thy servants as orphans
Whom Thou hast loved in Thy compassion
But send down on us thy holy spirit as Thou didst promise
Who will illumine our souls

After fulfilling the mystery of Thy dispensation
Thou did ascend before Thy disciples
Thou did humble Thyself for my sake
Now Thou has returned to the place Thou did not leave
Send down upon us Thy most Holy Spirit
Who will illumine our souls?

Without leaving the Father's bosom
Having lived with men as a man
Today Thou hast ascended in glory from the mount
Mercifully raising our fallen nature enthroning it with the Father
on high
The angelic hosts were amazed with awe seeing Thy great love
for man
With them we glorify Thy condescension to us
With them we glorify Thy ascension from us
By it Thou did fill Thy disciples and Thy mother with great joy
By their prayers and through Thy great mercy
Make us Thy chosen people worthy of this joy

(*Stikhera on "Lord I call," Great Vespers*)

CHAPTER ELEVEN

PENTECOST:
THE FEAST OF THE HOLY TRINITY

Blessed art Thou O Christ our God
Who hast revealed the fisherman as most wise
By sending down upon them the Holy Spirit
Through them Thou didst draw the world into Thy net
O lover of man glory to Thee.

(*Troparion for Feast of Pentecost*)

Fifty days after Pascha we celebrate the feast of Pentecost. The first Pentecost is recounted in the Book of Acts which is also the epistle reading for this feast:

> When the day of Pentecost had come they were all together in one place. And suddenly a loud sound came from heaven like the rush of a mighty wind and it filled all the house where they were sitting. And there appeared to them tongues as of fire, distributed and resting on each one of them. And they were all filled with the Holy Spirit and began to speak in other tongues, as the Spirit gave them utterance. Now there were dwelling in Jerusalem Jews, devout men from every nation under heaven. And at this sound the multitude came together, and they were bewildered, because each one heard them speaking in his own language. And they were amazed and wondered saying, "Are not all of these who are speaking Galileans? And how is it that we hear each of us in his own native language?" (Acts 2:1–4).

The apostles were gathered together in the upper room in Jerusalem in order to celebrate the feast of Pentecost. Pentecost is often referred to as the birthday of the Church since we commemorate the beginning or birth of the proclamation of the Gospel to the world. Pentecost however was not a new celebration during the time of Jesus but has ancient roots in the Old Testament. The Old Testament refers to Pentecost as being the feast of the first fruits of the harvest or the feast of weeks since it came during the late spring and early summer months:

> Three times in the year you shall keep a feast to me. You shall keep the feast of unleavened bread; as I commanded you, you shall eat unleavened bread for seven days at the appointed time in the month of Abib, for in it you came out of Egypt. None shall appear before me empty handed. You shall keep the feast of the harvest, of the first fruits of your labor, of what you sow in the field. You shall keep the feast of the ingathering at the end of the year, when you gather in from the filed the fruit of you labor" (Exodus 23:14–17. See also Deuteronomy 16:9–12).

> And you shall count from the morrow after the Sabbath, from the day that you brought the sheaf of the wheat offering, seven full weeks shall they be, counting fifty to the morrow after the seventh Sabbath; then you shall present a cereal offering of new grain to the Lord. You shall bring from your dwellings two loaves of bread to be waved, made of two tenths of an ephah; they shall be of the fine flour, they shall be baked with leaven, as first fruits to the Lord. And you shall present with the bread seven lambs a year old without blemish, and one young bull, and two rams, they shall be a burnt offering and their drink offerings, an offering of fire, a pleasing odor to the Lord. And you shall offer one male goat for a sin offering, and two male lambs a year old as a sacrifice of peace offerings. And the priest shall wave them with the bread of the first fruits as a wave offering before the Lord, with the two lambs, they shall be holy to the Lord for the priest. And you shall make proclamation on the same day; you shall hold a holy convocation; you shall do no laborious work: it is a statute forever in all your dwellings throughout your generations (Leviticus 23:15–21).

Scholars tell us that Pentecost was also referred to as the feast of weeks and commemorated the first harvesting of the crops during the late spring and early summer months. It was a seven week celebration and on the last day there was a great celebration for the feast, hence the name "Pentecost" which means fifty as we have it in our Pentagon building in Washington, DC, the five sided building which houses our military leaders and offices.

However, while Pentecost celebrated the first early summer harvest, in Christian terms it is a commemoration of the outpouring of the Holy Spirit upon the apostles which is a fulfillment of the prophecy of Joel which is also read at the service of Great Vespers on the eve of Pentecost:

> And the last days it shall be, God declares, that I will pour out My Spirit upon all flesh, and your sons and daughters shall prophesy, and your young men shall see visions, and your old men shall dream dreams; yea, and on My menservants and My maidservants in those days I will pour out my Spirit, and they shall prophesy. And I will show wonders in the heaven above and signs on the earth beneath, blood, and fire, and vapor of smoke; the sun shall be turned into darkness and the moon into blood before the day of the Lord comes, the great and manifest day. And it shall be that whoever calls on the name of the Lord shall be saved (Acts 2:17–20. See also Joel 2:23–32).

Peter and the other disciples were not drunk as people supposed they were but were full of the Holy Spirit. They began to speak in different tongues, preaching in the various languages of the Roman Empire which are listed in the previous passage, Parthians, Medes, Elmaites, residents of Cappadocia, Pontus, and Asia (Acts 2:9). In other words everyone heard the Gospel being preached in their own native tongue. The feast of Pentecost is a feast of preaching, the apostles, filled with the Holy Spirit received the gift of proclaiming the Gospel to the whole world. However, earlier in the Old Testament, in Genesis, we encounter the building of the tower of Babel and the problem with language:

> Now the whole earth had one language and few words. And as men migrated from the east, they found a plain in the land of Shinar and settled there. And they said to one another, "Come, let us make bricks, and burn them thoroughly." And they had brick for stone, and bitumen for mortar. Then they said, "Come,

let us build ourselves a city, and a tower with its top in the heavens, and let us make a name for ourselves, lest we be scattered abroad upon the face of the whole earth." And the Lord came down to see the city and the tower, which the sons of men had built. And the Lord said, "Behold, they are one people, and they have all one language; and this is only the beginning of what they will do; and nothing that they propose to do will now be impossible for them. Come, let us go down, and there confuse their language, that they may not understand one another's speech." So the Lord scattered them abroad from there over the face of all the earth, and they left off building the city. Therefore its name was called Ba'bel, because there the Lord confused the language of all the earth; and from there the Lord scattered them abroad over the face of all the earth (Genesis 11:1-9).

These gifts of tongues are referred to as "tongues of fire" which hearkens earlier to the Gospel of Luke, where John the Baptist says that while he baptizes with water, Jesus will baptize you with the Holy Spirit and with fire, "I baptize you with water; but He who is mightier than I is coming, the thong of whose sandals I am not worthy to untie; He will baptize you with the Holy Spirit and with fire" (Luke 3:16).

During Pentecost we commemorate the outpouring of the Holy Spirit upon the Church and recall the importance of Jesus' final words to His disciples that His disciples must continue in His preaching and teaching ministry until He comes again. Thus, at Pentecost we are encouraged to once again reaffirm our baptismal calling to live according to the Word of God and proclaim it the best we can in both our words and our deeds as we are witnesses to the death and resurrection of Jesus.

This Feast of Pentecost which is celebrated fifty days after the feast of Pascha reminds us that we are living in the "end times" since we have the Holy Spirit poured out upon us. The end times refers to God's judgment as we affirm and confess in the creed, "and He will come to judge the living and the dead and His kingdom shall have no end." This judgment is a powerful image since we are held accountable for the Gospel. During the service of Great Vespers for Pentecost, which is celebrated the evening before, we read the following verses from the prophet Ezekiel:

> For I will take you from the nations, and gather you from the countries, and bring you into your own land. I will sprinkle clean water upon you, and you shall be clean from all your uncleanesses, and from all your idols and I will cleanse you. A new heart I will give you, and a new spirit I will put within you; and I will take out of your flesh the heart of stone and give you a heart of flesh. And I will put my spirit within you, and cause you to walk in my statutes and be careful to observe my ordinances. You shall dwell in the land which I gave to your fathers; and you shall be my people, and I will be your God (Ezekiel 36:22–28).

Ezekiel's words are very powerful since they remind us of the continuous temptation to worship idols and false gods even in our own day and age. Very often we are just like the Israelites, turning away from the Lord, seeking after a god which we construct with our own imagination and worship them on altars which we build to honor them. Often times our heart is a heart of stone, refusing to listen and follow Jesus. Yet all is not forsaken, since the Lord loves us so much he has sent His Spirit upon us in order to lead us back to repentance and to walk the narrow path towards the Kingdom. In other words we have been given a new lease on life so to speak, another chance to follow Jesus as He leads us to the knowledge of the truth which is God Himself. May we always remain steadfast in our faith, seeking the will of God, offering prayer and praise to Him who reigns from His throne forever and ever. "Amen. Come, Lord Jesus" (Revelations 22:20):

> The nations did not know the power of the Holy Spirit
> Which came upon Your apostles O Lord,
> So they mistook the foreign tongues for drunkenness
> But we are strengthened by the apostles
> So we ceaselessly pray to You, O loving God,
> Do not take your Holy Spirit from us.
>
> The coming of the Holy Spirit
> Filled Your apostles, O Lord,

And made them speak in foreign tongues
To the faithless this wonder was but drunkenness,
But to the faithful it brings salvation
We pray to You, O loving God,
Make us worthy of such enlightenment

O heavenly King,
The Comforter, the Spirit of Truth
You are everywhere and fill all things
Treasury of blessings
And giver of Life
Come and abide in us
Cleanse us from every impurity
And save our souls, O good one.

(*Stikhera on the Aposticha for Great Vespers*)

After the feast of Pentecost the apostles were sent out of Jerusalem in order to proclaim the Gospel of the Kingdom and to baptize. They went out of Jerusalem to Judea and to the rest of the world. This small detail is very important because they started in the holy city of Jerusalem, the center of the Jewish world. Then they went out to Judea, to the place where the Jews lived, and then to the rest of the world which is the area of the Gentiles. So we see that they started preaching the Gospel in the heart of Judaism which was Jerusalem then to the Gentiles. We see this progression throughout the rest of the book of Acts. Acts retells the story of the first Christians and the ministry of the apostles who were sent out preaching and baptizing all nations. This new religion was referred to as the "Way" and we know that in Antioch these people were first called "Christians" (Acts 11).

At the conclusion of the Divine Liturgy for Pentecost it is customary for parishes to serve what is called the "Vespers of Pentecost with Kneeling Prayers." This is the first time since Holy Week that we kneel again in a sign of humility. The fifty days of celebrating Pascha are over and we are kneeling, asking God for forgiveness and repentance. The three long prayers refer to the awesome gift of God's grace and the importance of repentance. The hymns from the Vesper service also call to mind the gift of the Holy Spirit and its vivifying power in creation:

Today in the city of David
All nations behold glorious wonder
When the disciple of Christ gathered together
And the Holy Spirit came down in tongues of fire
As Luke, inspired of God records
A sound came like the rushing of a mighty wind
It filled all the house where they were sitting
And they all began to proclaim strange words
Strange doctrines, strange teachings, of the Holy Trinity

The Holy Spirit was, is, and ever will be
Without beginning, without ending
Always ranked and numbered with the Father and the Son
He is life and the giver of life
He is light and the giver of light
All good and the fountain of goodness
Through him the Father is known and the Son glorified
Through him all people proclaim one power, one ranking,
One worship of the Holy Trinity

The Holy Spirit is light and life
A living fountain of spiritual gifts
The spirit of wisdom and understanding
All knowing, upright, good He leads us and washes away our sins
He is God and he makes us gods
He is fire proceeding from fire
Speaking and acting and distributing gifts
Through him all the prophets, martyrs, and apostles are crowned
Strange account, strange and wonderful sight
Fire is divided for distributing gifts

(*Stikhera on "Lord I call," Great Vespers*)

CHAPTER TWELVE

THE TRANSFIGURATION OF OUR LORD AND GOD AND SAVIOR JESUS CHRIST

(AUGUST 6)

Thou wast transfigured on the Mount O Christ God,
Revealing Thy glory to Thy disciples as far as they could bear it.
Let Thine everlasting light shine upon us sinners
Through the prayers of the Theotokos!
O Giver of Light glory to Thee!

(Troparion for the Feast of the Transfiguration)

Several times throughout the Gospels Jesus forewarns His disciples about the cost of discipleship as He predicts the approaching end of His own life, "If any man would come after Me, let him deny himself, take up his cross and follow Me. For whoever would save his life will lose it, and whoever loses his life for My sake will find it. For what will it profit a man, if he gains the whole world and forfeits his life?" (Matthew 16:24–26. See also Mark 8:34–9:1; Luke 9:23–27). In chapter 10 of Matthew's Gospel, Jesus instructs His disciples that they are not supposed to take bags or purses or material goods with them on their missionary journeys because God the Father will provide for their daily sustenance, "Therefore, I tell you, do not be anxious about your life, what you shall eat or what you shall drink, nor about your body, what you shall put on. Is not life more than food, and the body more than clothing? Look at the birds of the air; they neither sow nor reap nor gather into barns, and yet your heavenly Father feeds them" (Matthew 5:21–26; 10:1–23). In other words, they are supposed to be content with their current material possessions and should not be worried about building up earthly treasures a warning He also tells His disciples in the parable of the man who wants to build bigger barns for his treasures (Luke). In this reading from Matthew Jesus also warns His disciples to beware of the Jewish leaders who will persecute and arrest them, put them on trial, and condemn them to death.

The Gospel reading for the feast of the Transfiguration is from the Gospel of Matthew. Jesus takes with Him three disciples; Peter, James and John along with Him to a mountain. Matthew does not specifically mention the name of the mountain but Tradition states that it is Mount Tabor, which is approximately eleven miles west of the Sea of Galilee. Mount Tabor is mentioned in the Old Testament as a border location for three tribes; Zebulun, Issachar, and Naphtali (Joshua 19:22). Also, the mountain is mentioned in Judges 4:16 when the prophetess Deborah told Barak to go to Tabor and attack Sisera and the Canaanites. While the mountain is not specifically mentioned as "Tabor", 2 Peter makes reference to a mountain upon which Jesus took the three disciples. In the ancient world mountains were points of contact between earth and heaven. In Greek and Roman mythology we hear about Mount Olympus the home of the gods. In the Old Testament we hear about several mountains especially Mount Sinai where Moses received the Ten Commandments. In the Gospel of Matthew Jesus leads His disciples and the crowds to a high mountain where He delivers the Sermon on the Mount (Matthew 5–7). In the Gospels Jesus goes to the Mount of Olives and preaches about the coming destruction of Jerusalem. Even today tall mountains, such as Mount Everest and Mount Shasta, seem almost to "pierce the sky" with their tall snow capped peaks.

However, together with Peter, James, and John Matthew also tells us that Jesus was not alone on the mountain-top, Moses and Elijah, two important figures in the Old Testament are also with Him. Moses began his life in a humble manner, his parents were Israelites and were enslaved in Egypt, and since they were slaves they wanted to save their child from this terrible situation They put their child Moses in a basket and let him float down the river where Pharaohs' daughter took him in as her own. He was raised in Pharaoh's household and became a great leader (Exodus 2:1–23). However, for no apparent reason God chose Moses to be the leader of the Israelites:

> And the angel of the Lord appeared to him in a flame of fire out of the midst of a bush; and he looked, and lo, the bush was burning, yet it was not consumed. And Moses said, "I will turn aside and see this great sight, why the bush is not burnt. When the Lord saw that he turned aside to see, God called him out of the bush, "Moses, Moses!" And he said, "Here am I." Then he said, "do not come near; put off your shoes from your feet, for the place of which you are standing is holy ground." And he said, "I am the God of your father, the God of Abraham, the God of Isaac, and the God of Jacob." And Moses hid his face, for he was afraid to look at God" (Exodus 3:2–6).

The rest of the Exodus story recalls Moses leading the Israelites through the Red Sea to the Promised Land as well as receiving the Ten Commandments on Mount Sinai, "And having risen early in the morning, Moses went up to Mount Sinai, as the Lord had told him. And the Lord descended in a cloud, and Moses stood there before Him and called out in the name of the Lord. And the Lord passed by before his face, and called out, 'The Lord God, compassionate and merciful, long-suffering, greatly merciful, and true.' And Moses, making haste, stooped down to the earth and worshipped the Lord" (Exodus 34:8).

The other person mentioned with Jesus is Elijah who is mentioned in 1 and 2 Kings, was a prophet in the Old Testament. He prophesied to King Ahab that there would be a drought for three years. He later is fed by ravens from the sky, and raises a widow's son from the dead. Elijah also confronts Ahab by challenging him to a contest; whether the pagan god Baal or the biblical God Yahweh will make it rain. Elijah wins the contest when God sends a lightning bolt and consumes the offering which Elijah has offered. In the New Testament, some people think that Jesus is indeed Elijah returned again, "And who do men say that the Son of man is?" and they said, "Some say John the Baptist, others say Elijah, and others Jeremiah or one of the prophets"

(Matthew 16:14). Some people even thought that John the Baptist was Elijah, "and they asked him, 'What then? Are you Elijah?' He said, 'I am not.' 'Are you a prophet?' and he answered, 'No.'" (John 1:21). Like Moses, God also appeared to Elijah in His glory and splendor:

> And there he came to a cave, and lodged there; and behold, the word of the Lord came to him, and he said to him, "What are you doing here, Elijah?" He said, "I have been very jealous for the Lord, the God of hosts, for the people of Israel have forsaken thy covenant, thrown down the altars, and slain thy prophets with the sword; and I, even I only, am left, and they seek my life to take it away." And he said, "go forth, and stand upon the mount before the Lord." And behold the Lord passed by and a strong wind rent the mountains, and broke in pieces the rocks before the Lord, but h Lord was not in the wind; and after the wind an earthquake, but the Lord was not in the earthquake, and after the earthquake a fire; but the Lord was not in the fire, and after the fire a still small voices. And when Elijah heard it, he wrapped his face in the mantle and went out and stood at the entrance of the cave, and behold, there came a voice to him and said, "What are you doing here, Elijah," and he said, "I have been very jealous for the Lord, the God of hosts for the people of Israel have forsaken thy covenant, thrown down thy altars, and slain thy prophets with the sword; and I, even I only, am left; and they seek my life, to take it away." And the Lord said to him, "Go, return on your way to the wilderness of Damascus; and when you arrive, you shall anoint Hazael to be king over Syria" (1 Kings 19:9–16).

The fact that both Moses and Elijah are seen together point to the fact that Jesus fulfils both the law and the prophets. The Scriptures are replete with numerous references to Jesus' prophetic ministry, preaching the gospel of repentance and forgiveness of sins to the people. Philip told his brother Nathaniel that this Jesus is the one whom both the law and prophets spoke about, "We have found Him of whom Moses in the law and also the prophets wrote, Jesus of Nazereth, the son of Joseph" (John 1:45). Jesus wears simple clothes, confronts the Jewish religious and political authorities, supports the widow and the orphan, and challenges people to a new way of life; typical teachings of the Old Testament prophets.

As Jesus was on top of the mountain the Gospels recall that His face shone brighter than the sun and His clothes were white as light. Jesus' face is transformed, radiating the glory of his Father. We have a glimpse of this in the beginning of the Gospel of John, "We have beheld His glory, glory as of the only Son from the Father" (John 1:14). Jesus' transformed face also echoes back to Moses on Mount Sinai as Moses face too reflected the glory of God:

> And when Moses had finished speaking with them, he put a veil on his face; but whenever Moses went in before the Lord to speak with Him, he took the veil off, until he came out; and when he came out and told the people of Israel what was commanded, the people of Israel saw the face of Moses, that the skin of Moses' face shone; and Moses would put the veil upon his face again, until he went in to speak with him" (Exodus 34:33–35. See also 2 Corinthians 3:12–18).

Ironically Peter, James, and John are the three disciples which are mentioned quite frequently throughout the Gospels and whom do not get high marks for their faith either. Peter denies Jesus three times, who sinks in the sea after he takes his eyes off Jesus and worries about the wind and the waves around him, and who does not believe the Myrrhbearing women when they tell him that Jesus has been raised from the dead. On the other hand, James and John, the sons of Zebedee are seen bickering about who will get the best places in the kingdom. Jesus rebukes them for their ridiculous talk and reminds them that it is not his place to give them the best seats in the Kingdom, that is only reserved for God. These three disciples seem to be the most stubborn and arrogant of the bunch, yet Jesus takes these three with Him on the mountain.

The disciples see Jesus' face turn as bright as the son and they also hear a voice from heaven which says, "This is My beloved Son with whom I am well pleased, listen to Him" (Matthew 17:5). The importance that the voice from heaven specifically identifies Jesus as His beloved Son is a reminder of Jesus' true power and authority as we hear in the Gospel of John, "Jesus said to them, 'If God were your Father, you would love Me, for I proceeded and came forth from God; I came not on My own accord, but He sent Me. Why do you not understand what I say? It is because you cannot bear to hear My word'" (John 8:43). The voice is also important because it is also connected with the voice from heaven which was heard at Jesus' baptism in the Jordan River, "And when Jesus was baptized, He went up immediately from the water, and behold, the heavens were opened and He saw the Spirit of God descending like a dove, and alighting on Him; and lo, a voice from heaven, saying, 'This is My beloved Son, with whom I am well pleased'" (Matthew 3:16–17; Mark 1:9–11; Luke 3:21–22; John 1:31–34). Furthermore, throughout the prophetic writings the identification of Jesus as the "beloved Son" marks the beginning of Jesus' teaching ministry in the Galilee area and confirms His role as the teacher. The voice from the Transfiguration account includes the phrase "listen to Him," which is a requirement on the part of Jesus' followers. They have to listen to Him which also means to obey Him as well because Jesus is teaching them about the kingdom of God.

The disciples of Jesus are supposed to listen to Jesus because Jesus is the very Word of God which came from God the Father, He is the incarnate Word, "In the beginning was the Word and the Word was with God and the Word was God" (John 1:1). The emphasis on the teaching aspect of Jesus' ministry is essential. Earlier in Matthew Jesus instructs His disciples in the Sermon on the Mount to follow His instructions about prayer, fasting, almsgiving as well as repentance and forgiveness of sins. Later in Matthew He literally blasts the hypocrisy of the Pharisees and Sadducees, the "teachers" of the community for their lack of true teaching:

> Then said Jesus to the crowds and to His disciples, "The scribes and the Pharisees sit on Moses' seat; so practice and observe whatever they tell you, but not what they do; for they preach, but do not practice. They bind heavy burdens, hard to bear, and lay them on men's shoulders; but they themselves will not move

them with their finger. They do all their deeds to be seen by men; for they make their phylacteries broad and their fringes long, and they love the place of honor at feasts and the best seats in the synagogues" (Matthew 23:1–6).

This warning is meant for the disciples that they are to be very careful about what they say since they are in fact speaking with the same authority as Moses as Jesus mentions "Moses' seat," which is the seat of teaching. The teachings, of course, are the commandments and law of God, otherwise known as the Gospel. This Gospel teaching is a word of instruction that Paul emphasizes throughout his epistles. The instruction, according to the epistle to the Hebrews is like a two edge sword which cuts the very bones and sinews bringing the hearer to repentance and change of heart, "For the word of God is living and active, sharper than any two edged sword, piercing to the division of soul and spirit, of joints and marrow, and discerning the thoughts and intentions of the heart. And before him no creature is hidden, but all are open and laid bare to the eyes of him with whom we have to do" (Hebrews 4:11–13). In other words the fact that Peter, James, and John wanted to make three booths or tents in order to remain on the mountain is not a good thing. The fact that Jesus was radiating the glory of God, which is also connected with the glory in the Temple in Jerusalem, and the fact that the voice from heaven confirms that they are supposed to listen to Jesus' teaching, means that there is work to be accomplished. Jesus already predicted that He is headed towards Jerusalem in order to be put to death and He warned His disciples about that already as well in Matthew chapter 10. Here they are once again encouraged to hear and obey His teaching which is the gospel of faith, which is also confirmed with the fact that Moses and Elijah, representing the Law and the Prophets, are also with Jesus on the mountain. These themes of course are beautifully reflected in the hymns from the Vesper service which we celebrate for the Feast of Transfiguration:

Before thy crucifixion O Lord
The mountain became as heaven and a cloud spread itself out to form a tabernacle

When Thou wast transfigured and the Father testified unto Thee
Peter with James and John were there
Who were to be present with thee also at the time of Thy betrayal
That having beheld thy wonders they should not be afraid before
Thy suffering

Grant in Thy great mercy that we too may be counted worthy to
venerate these Thy sufferings in peace.

Before Thy crucifixion O Lord,
Taking the disciples up into a high mountain
Thou wast transfigured before them,
Shining upon them with the bright beams of Thy power:
From love of mankind and in Thy sovereign might,
Thy desire it was to show them the splendor of the Resurrection.
Grant that we too in peace may be counted worthy of this splendor,
O God
For Thou art merciful and lovest mankind.

The Mountain that once was gloomy and veiled in smoke
Now has become venerable and holy
For Thy feet, O Lord, have stood upon it.
Thy dread Transfiguration, the mystery hidden before the ages
Has been made manifest in the last times to Peter, John, and James
They cold not endure Thy shining countenance and bright
garments
They fell to the ground upon their faces
Seized with astonishment and wonder
They saw Moses and Elijah talking with thee of the things that
should befall Thee
A voice in testimony came from the Father:
"This is my beloved Son in whom I am well pleased, hear Him
He it is who grants the world great mercy"

Prefiguring Thy resurrection, O Christ our God
Thou hast taken with Thee in Thy ascent to Mount Tabor
Thy three disciples, Peter, James and John
When Thou was transfigured, O savior
Mount Tabor was covered with light
Thy disciples, O word, cast themselves down upon the ground
They were unable to gaze upon the form that none may see

The angels ministered in fear and trembling
The earth quaked and the heavens shook
As they beheld upon the Lord of glory.

(*Stikhera on "Lord I call," Great Vespers*)

CHAPTER THIRTEEN

THE DORMITION (FALLING ASLEEP) OF THE MOST HOLY THEOTOKOS
(August 6)

In Giving Birth
You preserved your virginity
In falling asleep you did not forsake the world O Theotokos
You were translated to life
O Mother of Life
And through your prayers deliver our souls from death!

(*Troparion for the Dormition of the Holy Theotokos*)

The last feast day according to the Orthodox liturgical calendar is the feast of the Dormition of the Theotokos which is celebrated on August 15. This feast day is preceded by a fifteen-day fasting period which begins on August 1 and lasts until the Divine Liturgy celebrated on the feast itself. Some parishes serve the Paraklesis service on the week-days during this time, other parishes serve the Akathist to the Mother of God, asking for her prayers and intercessions. This last feast of the Church year is an important one because it celebrates the death of Mary. Some parishes even have a winding sheet with the icon of Mary lying in the grave, similar if not identical to the winding sheet or *epitaphios* that we use on Holy Friday which depicts Jesus in the grave.

The Scriptures do not offer us an account of Mary's death. The last time we hear about Mary is at the feast of Pentecost when she is with the other disciples in the upper room when the Holy Spirit comes upon them in the form of fiery tongues. Paul makes a passing reference to her in his epistle to the Galatians, but aside from those two occasions nothing else is mentioned. However, if we look at one of the apocryphal gospels, particularly the apocryphal Gospel of John we have recorded her death which is expressed in a dramatic fashion:

> The apostles said all these things to the holy mother of God, why they had come, and in what way; and she stretched her hands to heaven and prayed, saying: I adore, and praise, and glorify Your much to be praised name, O Lord, because You have looked upon the lowliness of Your handmaiden, and because You that are mighty hast done great things for me; and, behold, all generations shall count me blessed (Luke 1:48). And after the prayer she said to the apostles: Cast incense, and pray. And when they had prayed, there was thunder from heaven, and there came a fearful voice, as if of chariots; and, behold, a multitude of a host of angels and powers, and a voice, as if of the Son of man, was heard, and the seraphim in a circle round the house where the holy, spotless mother of God and virgin was lying, so that all who were in Bethlehem beheld all the wonderful things, and came to Jerusalem and reported all the wonderful things that had come to pass. And it came to pass, when the voice was heard, that the sun and the moon suddenly appeared about the house; and an assembly of the first-born saints stood beside the house where the mother of the Lord was lying, for her honour and glory. And I beheld also that many signs came to pass, the blind seeing, the deaf hearing, the lame walking, lepers cleansed, and those possessed by unclean spirits cured; and every one who was under disease and sickness, touching the outside of the wall of the house where she was lying, cried out: Holy Mary, who brought forth Christ our God, have mercy upon us. And they were straightway cured. And great multitudes out of every country living in Jerusalem for the sake of prayer, having heard of the signs that had come to pass in Bethlehem through the mother of the Lord, came to the place seeking the cure of various diseases, which also they obtained. And there was joy unspeakable on that day among the multitude of those who had been cured, as well as of those who looked on, glorifying Christ our God and His mother. And all Jerusalem from Bethlehem kept festival with psalms and spiritual songs.

The beautiful hymnography for this feast is also based on this account from John. The Dormition feast is a beautiful one as it celebrates her death. The Gospel reading for this feast is taken from the Gospel of Luke chapters ten and eleven. Most of the time the Gospel readings are read in order, however, the Gospel reading for this feast is comprised of two chapters from the Gospel of Luke:

> Now as they went on their way, He entered a village; and a woman named Martha received Him into her house. And she had a sister called Mary, who sat at the Lord's feet and listened to His teaching. But Martha was distracted with much serving; and she went to Him and said, "Lord, do You not care that my sister has left me to serve alone? Tell her then to help me." But the Lord answered her, "Martha, Martha, you are anxious and troubled about many things; one thing is needful. Mary has chosen the good portion, which shall not be taken away from her. And he said this, a woman in the crowd raised her voice and said to Him, "Blessed is the womb that bore you, and the breasts that you sucked!" But He said, "Blessed rather are those who hear the word of God and keep it!" (Luke 10:38–42; 11:27–28).

Many Gospel readings are read in order, however, the three feasts of Mary have a Gospel reading from Luke that is comprised from two different chapters. Immediately before this particular Gospel reading Jesus tells the parable of the Good Samaritan which serves as the immediate context for this passage. This theme of service and sacrificial love. Then we hear about Mary and Martha, two sisters who are also mentioned in John 11 in context their brother Lazarus who was dead. Mary was sitting at Jesus' feet listening to His teaching and her sister Martha was in the kitchen worrying about serving the Master:

> Now as they went on their way, He entered a village; and a woman named Martha received him into her house. And she had a sister called Mary, who sat at the Lord's feet and listened to His teaching. But Martha was distracted with much serving; and she went to Him and said, "Lord, do You not care that my sister has left me to serve alone? Tell her then to help me." But the Lord answered her, "Martha, Martha, you are anxious and troubled about many things; one thing is needful. Mary has chosen the good portion, which shall not be taken away from her" (Luke 10:38-42).

Very often people say that we are supposed to be both like Mary and Martha, both in learning and serving. Others speak about having a Mary heart in a Martha world which usually means having a heart open to Jesus in a hectic and crazy world. The important trajectory in this short passage is that Mary chose the "good portion" which is sitting at Jesus' feet listening to His teaching. The primacy of the "word of teaching" here is essential because it appears throughout the New Testament. Likewise, Jesus is seen teaching the Word of God in the synagogue earlier in Luke chapter 4. At the end of Luke Jesus opens the minds of His disciples on the road to Emmaus and interprets the Scripture to them. In the Book of Acts we see a growing problem among the widows who were being neglected in the distribution of food and material possessions. The disciples however did not want to give up "preaching the word" in order to serve. In other words, the primacy in this passage is the preaching of the Gospel:

> Now in these days when the disciples were increasing in number, the Hellenists murmured against the Hebrews because their widows were neglected in the daily distribution. And the twelve summoned the body of the disciples and said, "It is not right that we should give up preaching the word of God to serve tables. Therefore, brethren, pick out from among you seven men of good repute, full of the Spirit and of wisdom, whom we may appoint to this duty. But we will devote ourselves to prayer and to the ministry of the word." And what they said pleased the whole multitude, and they chose Stephen, a man full of faith and of the Holy Spirit, and Philip, and Proch'orus, and Nica'nor, and Ti'mon, and Par'menas, and Nicola'us, a proselyte of Antioch. These they set before the apostles, and they prayed and laid their hands upon them. And the word of God increased; and the number of the disciples multiplied greatly in Jerusalem, and a great many of the priests were obedient to the faith (Acts 6:1–7).

Likewise, in the Gospel lesson from Luke Jesus acknowledges Mary's devotion to his teaching rather than Martha's overly anxious serving. This is also supported by the fact that the second portion of this Gospel reading, from Luke chapter 11 where an unnamed woman in

the crowd congratulates Jesus' human family by blessing His mother, "And as He said this a woman in the crowd raised her voice and
said to Him, 'Blessed is the womb that bore You, and the breasts that
You sucked!'" (Luke 11:27). In other words she is congratulating his
family lineage and family of origin. Yet Jesus responds to her by saying, "Blessed rather are those who hear the word of God and keep
it!" (Luke 11:28), which is nearly identical to an earlier statement in
Luke where Jesus says, "My mother and My brothers are those who
hear the word of God and do it" (Luke 8:21). Twice then in the same
reading, with Mary and Martha and then with this unnamed woman,
Jesus gives preference to hearing and obeying the Word of God. Her
place in the Church is always in function of her son Jesus and His
kingship over all creation which is seen in the hymnography from the
feast day:

> O marvelous wonder
> The source of life is laid in the tomb
> And the tomb itself becomes a ladder to heaven
> Make glad O Gethsemane, Thou sacred abode of the Mother of God
> Come, O you faithful and with Gabriel to lead us let us cry:
> Hail, Thou who art full of grace the Lord is with Thee
> Granting the world through Thee great mercy.
>
> Glorious are Thy mysteries O pure lady
> Thou wast made the throne of the Most High
> And today Thou art translated from earth to heaven
> Thy glory is full of majesty shining with grace in divine brightness
> O virgins ascend on high with the Mother of the King
> Hail Thou art full of grace the Lord is with Thee
> Granting the world through Thee great mercy.
>
> The dominions and the thrones
> The rulers, the principalities, and the powers
> The cherubim and fearful seraphim
> Glorify your Dormition
> And those who dwell on earth rejoice
> Adorned by your divine glory
> Kings fall down and sing with the archangels
> "Hail, O full of grace, the Lord is with you

Through you granting the world great mercy

Sing O people
Sing the praises of the Mother of our God
For today she delivers her soul, full of light
Into the immaculate hands of him
Who was made incarnate of her without seed
She entreats him without ceasing
To grant the world peace and great mercy

By the royal command of God,
The divinely inspired apostles were caught up from over the world
Into thy clouds on high
Reaching your immaculate body, the source of life,
They saluted it with honor
The highest powers of heaven stood by with their own master
They accompanied your inviolate body that had held God
Seized with dread, they went on high before you
Unseen, they cried to the hosts above:
"Lo, the Queen of all, the maid of god, is nigh
Open wide the gates and receive above the world
The mother of the everlasting light
For through her the salvation of all mankind has come
We have not the strength to look upon her
We are unable to render honors worthy of her
For her excellence is past all understanding
Therefore, O most pure Theotokos
Living forever with your son, the king, the bringer of life
Pray without ceasing that your newborn people
May be guarded on every side and saved from all adversity
For we are under your protection
And we bless you in beauty and light unto ages of ages.

(*Stikhera on "Lord I call," Great Vespers*)

BIBLIOGRAPHY

GENERAL RESOURCES FOR FEAST DAYS:

Baggley, John. *Festival Icons for the Christian Year*. Crestwood, NY: St. Vladimir's Seminary Press, 2000.

Dunlop, Olga (trans.). *The Living God: A Catechism Volume 1 and 2*. Crestwood, NY: St. Vladimir's Seminary Press, 1996.

Hopko, Thomas. *The Lenten Spring*. Crestwood, NY: St. Vladimir's Seminary Press, 1983.

_____. *The Winter Pascha*. Crestwood, NY: St. Vladimir's Seminary Press, 1984.

Mother Mary and Archmandrite Kallistos Ware (trans.). *The Festal Menaion*. South Canaan, St. Tikhon's Seminary Press, 1969.

Schmemann, Alexander. *The Church Year: The Celebration of Faith Volume 2 and 3*. Crestwood, NY: St. Vladimir's Seminary Press, 1994/1995.

_____. *Great Lent: Journey to Pascha*. Crestwood, NY: St. Vladimir's Seminary Press, 1969.

Wybrew, Hugh *Orthodox Feasts of Jesus Christ and the Virgin Mary: Liturgical Texts with Commentary*. Crestwood, NY: St. Vladimir's Seminary Press, 2000.

GENERAL REFERENCES FOR SCRIPTURE STUDY:

Bianchi, Enzo. *Praying the Word: An Introduction to Lectio Divina.* Kalamazoo, MI: Cistercian Publications, 1998.

Johnson, Luke Timothy. *Living Jesus: Learning the Heart of the Gospel.* San Fransisco, CA: Harper Collins, 1999.

Mills, William C. *From Pascha to Pentecost: Reflections on the Gospel of John.* Rollinsford, NH: Orthodox Research Institute, 2004.

_____. *Prepare O Bethlehem: Reflections on the Gospel Readings for Nativity and Epiphany.* Rollinsford, NH: Orthodox Research Institute, 2005.

_____. *Baptize All Nations: Reflections on the Gospel of Matthew During the Pentecost Season.* Rollinsford, NH: Orthodox Research Institute, 2006.

_____. *A Light to the Gentiles: Reflections on the Gospel of Luke.* NY, iUniverse, 2007.

Royster, Archbishop Dmitri. *The Parables.* Crestwood, NY: St. Vladimir's Seminary Press, 1996.

_____. *The Miracles of Christ.* Crestwood, NY: St Vladimir's Seminary Press, 1999.

INTERNET RESOURCES FOR SCRIPTURE STUDY:

Orthodox Center for the Advancement of Biblical Studies:
www.ocabs.org

New Testament Gateway:
www.ntgateway.com

PBS Documentary "From Jesus To Christ":
www.pbs.org/wgbh/page/frontline/show/religion

CELEBRATING FEAST DAYS
IN THE HOME

Feast days reveal the corporate nature of Orthodox worship. The Church is primarily a community of faith which celebrates together our thanksgiving to God in worship. All feast days include numerous liturgical services Great Vespers or Vigil, Matins, and the Divine Liturgy. However, we are now living in an increasingly mobile society where many families have to make choices between Church, work, school, and other social activities. Most people do not live in a country village and have the opportunity walk to Church or live near Church. We are more suburban and lead hectic and busy lives ever than before. This of course is not necessarily the best way to live. One of the greatest challenges for families is how to keep the festal celebration alive in the home, especially if we cannot always attend the festal services due to work or other family obligations. In other words, we can still maintain a "festal atmosphere" or "festal celebration" at home since our families really are communities within communities. Below are several suggestions about how our families can keep the "feasts alive" and share the peace and joy in our domestic "Churches" wherever we find ourselves:

1. If possible, attend the feast day services at church. If the feast day involves blessing objects such as water, candles, fruit, or flowers bring these items to Church and have the children participate. Bring your child shopping with your for fruit or flowers or if you have a summer flower garden have them come with you and cut fresh flowers to bring to Church. At the feast of Epiphany have your children bring a small jar to

Church so they can take come Holy Water home with them. At the feast of the Meeting of the Lord have your children bring candles from home so that the candles can be blessed at the end of the service. These small gestures are actually ways that children learn about their faith. These symbols will remain with them for a lifetime.

2. Many families pray the "Lord's Prayer" before meals. During the festal period you can subsitute the "Lord's Prayer" with the festal tropraion which can be found at the beginning of each chapter of *Feasts of Faith*. Additional liturgical music for the feast days can be found on many national Church websites such as www.oca.org, www.goarch.org, or www.antiochian.org. You can always consult your local choir director or priest about how to obtain these hymns.

3. Purchase a set of icon prints for the feast days. Your parish bookstore can order them or you can go to a large national Orthodox bookstore like St. Vladimir's Seminary Bookstore, Light-N-Life, or Conciliar Press and ask them. Take a 4x6 or 5x7 picture frame and put a feast day icon in it. As each feast day goes by replace the small icon card inside the frame. Keep the frame somewhere where the children will see it such as the kitchen or kitchen table. Put a small candle in front of the frame during dinner time. Children learn by looking at pictures and this is a simple yet powerful way to be reminded of why we are celebrating this particular feast day.

4. Read the prescribed festal scripture readings together as a family, especially the gospel readings. If the children cannot read the parents can read the lessons to them. The scripture readings are listed in the appendix in the back of this book and also can be found on your parish calendar. Discuss the readings together as a family.

Families celebrate birthdays, anniversaries, retirements, and weddings, why not celebrate Church feast days too! Children love to celebrate and have parties there is no reason why families cannot keep the festal season alive in the home just as we do in the liturgical services. It only takes some planning and some creativity but with a little work and effort this is a great tradition to pass onto our children and grandchildren.

SCRIPTURE READINGS FOR FEAST DAYS ACCORDING TO THE ORTHODOX LITURGICAL CALENDAR

THE NATIVITY OF THE THEOTOKOS
Great Vespers: Genesis 28:10–17; Ezekiel 43:27–44:4;
    Proverbs 9:1–11
Matins: Luke 1:39–49, 56
Divine Liturgy: Philippians 2:5–11; Luke 10:38–42, 11:27–28

THE EXALTATION OF THE LIFE CREATING CROSS
Great Vespers: Exodus 15:22–16:1; Proverbs 3:11–18;
    Isaiah 60:11–16
Matins: John 12:28-36
Divine Liturgy: 1 Corinthians 1:18–24; John 19:6–11, 13–20,
    25-28, 30–35

THE ENTRANCE OF THE THEOTOKOS INTO THE TEMPLE
Great Vespers: Composite from Exodus 40, composite from
    1 Kings 7–8; Ezekiel 43:27–44:4
Matins: Luke 1:39–49, 56
Divine Liturgy: Hebrews 9:1–7; Luke 10:38–42, 11:27–28

THE NATIVITY OF OUR LORD AND SAVIOR JESUS CHRIST
Matins: Matthew 1:18-25
Divine Liturgy: Galatians 4:4-7, Matthew 1:1–12

The Theophany of Our Lord and Savior Jesus Christ
Matins: Mark 1:9–11
Divine Liturgy: Titus 2:11–14; Matthew 3:13–17

The Meeting of our Lord into the Temple
Great Vespers: Isaiah 6:1-12; Composite from Exodus 12, 13,
   Numbers 8, Leviticus 12; Composite from Isaiah 19:1, 3,
   4–5, 12, 16, 19–21
Matins: Luke 2:25–32
Divine Liturgy: Hebrews 7:7–17; Luke 2:22–40

The Annunciation of Our Most Holy Lady, the Theotokos and Ever-Virgin Mary
Great Vespers: Genesis 28:10–17; Ezekiel 43:27–44:4;
   Proverbs 9:1–11; Exodus 3:1–8; Proverbs 8:22–30
Matins: Luke 1:39–49, 56
Divine Liturgy: Hebrews 2:11–18; Luke 1:24–38

The Entry of Our Lord into Jerusalem
Great Vespers: Genesis 49:1–2, 8–12; Zephaniah 3:14–19;
   Zechariah 9:9–15
Matins: Matthew 21:1–11, 15–17
Divine Liturgy: Philippians 4:4–9; John 12:1–18

Pascha: The Resurrection of our Lord
Divine Liturgy: Acts 1:1–8; John 1:1–17

The Ascension of Our Lord
Great Vespers: Isaiah 2:2–3; Composite from Isaiah 62:10–63:3,
   7, 9; Composite from Zechariah 14:1, 4, 8–11
Matins: Mark 16:9–20
Divine Liturgy: Acts 1:1–12; Luke 24:36–53

Pentecost—Feast of the Holy Trinity
Great Vespers: Numbers 11:16–17, 24–29; Joel 2:23–32;
   Ezekiel 36:24–28
Matins: John 20:19–23
Divine Liturgy: Acts 2:1–11; John 7:37–52, 8:12

THE TRANSFIGURATION OF OUR LORD

Great Vespers: Exodus 24:12-18; Composite from
Exodus 33:11–23, 34:4–6, 8; II Kings 19:3–9, 11–13, 15, 16
Matins: Luke 9:28–36
Divine Liturgy: 2 Peter 1:10–19; Matthew 17:1–9

THE DORMITION OR FALLING ASLEEP OF OUR MOST HOLY LADY AND THEOTOKOS AND EVER-VIRGIN MARY

Great Vespers: Genesis: 28:10–17; Ezekiel 43:27–44:4;
Proverbs 9:1–11
Matins: Luke 1:39–49:56
Divine Liturgy: Philippians 2:5–11; Luke 10:38–42, 11:27–28

PATRISTIC TEXTS
ON THE FEAST DAYS

John Chrysostom (died 407)

John was born in Antioch in 347. Like Gregory, John had a classical education that included both rhetoric and philosophy. John studied under the direction of the great philosopher Libanius. When John returned to Antioch he befriended Bishop Meletius who baptized John and then ordained him to the diaconate. After baptism, Chrysostom entered the dessert for six years. He put himself under the care and guidance of Diodore of Tarsus, the famous Antiochene exegete. Diodore established a school for the learning and interpretation of scripture and was sought out as one of the greatest teachers of scripture in the Christian East. His students lived an austere lifestyle devoted to fasting and prayer with the remainder of time devoted to studying scripture.

Under the new bishop Flavian, John assisted in assisting the poor and needy, and even though he was a deacon, preached frequently in Church. In 398 John was appointed bishop in Constantinople where he found himself at the center of the Roman Empire. While in Constantinople John had different duties then when he was a priest yet he still continued to preach and teach as was his custom. As bishop, John's responsibilities were devoted the financial well being of the diocese as well as maintaining peace and concord among the clergy and local parish churches. John was the chief pastor in the capital city and therefore had much greater responsibilities then when he was a priest. However, while his obligations took him to various places and locations John always cared for his community and preached sermons about repentance, love, forgiveness, and salvation.

Throughout his ecclesiastical career at Antioch and Constanti-nople John devoted himself to preaching the gospel and ministering to the church of Christ. Chrysostom encountered a lot of resistance to the truth from the rich upper class of society and the political lead-ers. However, John's only weapon was gospel of Christ and he used it whenever he had the opportunity. The vast number of his sermons and homilies that survive testify to this fact. John certainly earned the name "golden mouth" and priests and pastors still look to him as an example of as a true pastor of Christ's flock. St. John is com-memorated on November 13 and on January 30 together with, Basil the Great and Gregory the Theologian.

For Further Reading:

St. John Chrysostom. *On Marriage and Family* translated by Cathe-rine P. Roth and David Anderson (Crestwood, NY: St. Vladimir's Seminary Press, 1986).

_____. *On Wealth and Poverty* translated by Catherine P. Roth (Crestwood, NY: St. Vladimir's Seminary Press, 1984).

_____. *Six Books on the Priesthood* translated by Graham Neville (Crestwood, NY: St Vladimir's Seminary Press, 1984).

_____. *Baptismal Instructions* translated Paul W. Harkins (Mahwah, NJ: Paulist Press, 1963).

_____. *On The Cult of the Saints* translated Wendy Mayer with Bro-wen Neil (Crestwood, NY: St. Vladimir's Seminary Press, 2006).

Wendy Mayer and Pauline Allen. *John Chrysostom* (NY: Routledge, 2000).

J. N. D Kelly. *Golden Mouth: The Story of John Chrysostom: Asectic, Preacher, Bishop* (Grand Rapids, MI: Baker Books, 1995).

Homily 4 on the Acts of the Apostles

"And when the day of Pentecost was fully come, they were all with one accord in one place. And suddenly there came a sound from heaven."

Do you perceive the type? What is this Pentecost? The time when the sickle was to be put to the harvest, and the ingathering was made. See now the reality, when the time was come to put in the sickle of the word: for here, as the sickle, keen-edged, came the Spirit down. For hear the words of Christ: "Lift up your eyes," He said, "and look on the fields, for they are white already to harvest." (John iv. 35) And again, "The harvest truly is great, but the laborers are few." (Matt. ix. 38.) But as the first-fruits of this harvest, He himself took [our nature], and bore it up on high. Himself first put in the sickle. Therefore also He calls the Word the Seed. "When," it says, "the day of Pentecost was fully come"): that is, when at the Pentecost, while about it, in short. For it was essential that the present events likewise should take place during the feast, that those who had witnessed the crucifixion of Christ, might also behold these. "And suddenly there came a sound from heaven." (v. 2.) Why did this not come to pass without sensible tokens? For this reason. If even when the fact was such, men said, "They are full of new wine," what would they not have said, had it been otherwise? And it is not merely, "there came a sound," but, "from heaven." And the suddenness also startled them, and brought all together to the spot. "As of a rushing mighty wind:" this betokens the exceeding vehemence of the Spirit. "And it filled all the house:" insomuch that those present both believed, and in this manner were shown to be worthy. Nor is this all; but what is more awful still, "And there appeared unto them," it says, "cloven tongues like as of fire." (v. 3.) Observe how it is always, "like as;" and rightly: that you may have no gross sensible notions of the Spirit. Also, "as it were of a blast:" therefore it was not a wind. "Like as of fire." For when the Spirit was to be made known to John, then it came upon the head of Christ as in the form of a dove: but now, when a whole multitude was to be converted, it is "like as of fire. And it sat upon each of them." This means, that it remained and rested upon them." For the sitting is significant of settledness and continuance.

Was it upon the twelve that it came? Not so; but upon the hundred and twenty. For Peter would not have quoted to no purpose the testimony of the prophet, saying, "And it shall come to pass in the last days, says the Lord God, I will pour out of My spirit upon all flesh: and your sons and your daughters shall prophesy, and your young men shall see visions, and your old men shall dream dreams." (Joel ii. 28.) "And they were all filled with the Holy Ghost." (v. 4.) For, that the effect may not be to frighten only, therefore is it both "with the Holy Ghost, and with fire. And began to speak with other tongues, as the Spirit gave them utterance." (Matt. iii. 11.) They receive no other sign, but this first; for it was new to them, and there was no need of any other sign. "And it sat upon each of them," says the writer. Observe now, how there is no longer any occasion for that person to grieve, who was not elected as was Matthias, "And they were all filled," he says; not merely received the grace of the Spirit, but "were filled. And began to speak with other tongues, as the Spirit gave them utterance." It would not have been said, *All*, the Apostles also being there present, unless the rest also were partakers. For were it not so, having above made mention of the Apostles distinctively and by name, he would not now have put them all in one with the rest. For if, where it was only to be mentioned that they were present, he makes mention of the Apostles apart, much more would he have done so in the case here supposed. Observe, how when one is *continuing in prayer*, when one is in charity, then it is that the Spirit draws near. It put them in mind also of another vision: for as fire did He appear also in the bush. "As the Spirit gave them utterance (Exod. iii. 2.) For the things spoken by them were, profound utterances. "And," it says, "there were dwelling at Jerusalem Jews, devout men." (v. 5.) The fact of their dwelling there was a sign of piety: that being of so many nations they should have left country, and home, and relations, and be abiding there. For, it says, "There were dwelling at Jerusalem Jews, devout men, out of every nation under heaven. Now when this was noised abroad, the multitude came together, and were confounded. (v. 6.) Since the event had taken place in a house, of course they came together from without. The multitude *was confounded*: was all in commotion. They marvelled; "Because that every man heard them speak in his own language. And they were amazed," it says, "and marvelled, saying one to another, Behold, are not all these which speak Galileans?" (v. 7–13.) They immediately turned their eyes towards the Apostles. "And how" (it follows) "hear we every man in our own tongue, wherein we were born? Parthians, and Medes, and Elamites, and the dwellers in Mesopotamia, and in Judea, and Cappadocia, in Pontus, and Asia, Phrygia, and Pamphylia, in Egypt, and in the parts of Libya about Cyrene:" mark how they run from east to west: "and strangers of Rome, Jews and proselytes, Cretes and Arabians, we do hear them speak in our tongues the wonderful works of God. And, they were all amazed, and were in doubt, saying one to another, What means this? Others mocking said, These men are full of new wine." O the excessive folly! O the excessive malignity! Why it was not even the season for that; for it was Pentecost. For this was what made it worse: that when those were confessing — men that were Jews, that were Romans, that were proselytes, yea perhaps that had crucified Him — yet these, after so great signs, say, "They are full of new wine!"

But let us look over what has been said from the beginning. (Recapitulation.) "And when the day of Pentecost," etc. "It filled," he says, "the house." That wind was a very pool of water. This betokened the copiousness, as the fire did the vehemence. This nowhere happened in the case of the Prophets: for to uninebriated souls such accesses are not attended with much disturbance; but "when they have well drunken," then indeed it is as here, but with the Prophets it is otherwise. (Ez. iii. 3.) The roll of a book is given him, and Ezekiel ate what he was about to utter. "And it became in his mouth," it is said, "as honey for sweetness." (And again the hand of God touches the tongue of another Prophet; but here it is the Holy Ghost Himself: (Jer. i. 9) so equal is He in honor with the Father and the Son.) And again, on the other hand, Ezekiel calls it "Lamentations, and mourning, and woe." (Ez. ii. 10.) To them it might well be in the form of a book; for they still needed similitudes. Those had to deal with only one nation, and with their own people; but these with the whole world, and with men whom they never knew. Also Elisha receives the grace through the medium of a mantle (2 Kings xiii.); another by oil, as David (1 Sam. xvi. 13); and Moses by fire, as we read of him at the bush. (Exod. iii. 2.) But in the present case it is not so; for the fire itself sat upon them. (But wherefore did the fire not appear so as to fill the house? Because they would have been terrified.) But the story shows, that it is the same here as there. For you are not to stop at this, that "there appeared unto them cloven tongues," but note that they were "of fire." Such a fire as this is able to kindle infinite fuel. Also, it is well said, *Cloven*, for they were from one root; that you may learn, that it was an operation sent from the Comforter.

But observe how those men also were first shown to be worthy, and then received the Spirit as worthy. Thus, for instance, David: what he did among the sheepfolds, the same he did after his victory and trophy; that it might be shown how simple and absolute was his faith. Again, see Moses despising royalty, and forsaking all, and after forty years taking the lead of the people (Exod. ii. 11); and Samuel occupied there in the temple (1 Sam. iii. 3); Elisha leaving all (1 Kings xix. 21); Ezekiel again, made manifest by what happened thereafter. In this manner, you see, did these also leave all that they had. They learned also what human infirmity is, by what they suffered; they learned that it was not in vain they had done these good works. Even Saul, having first obtained witness that he was good, thereafter received the Spirit. But in the same manner as here did none of them receive. Thus Moses was the greatest of the Prophets, yet he, when others were to receive the Spirit, himself suffered diminution. But here it is not so; but just as fire kindles as many flames as it will, so here the largeness of the Spirit was shown, in that each one received a fountain of the Spirit; as indeed He Himself had foretold, that those who believe in Him, should have "a well of water springing up into everlasting life."

(John iv. 14.) And good reason that it should be so. For they did not go forth to argue with Pharaoh, but to wrestle with the devil. But the wonder is this, that when sent they made no objections; they said not, they were "weak in voice, and of a slow tongue." (Exod. iv. 10.) For Moses had taught them better. They said not, they were too young. (Jer. i. 6.) Jeremiah had made them wise. And yet they had heard of many fearful things, and much greater than were theirs of old time; but they feared to object. — And because they were angels of light, and ministers of things above ["Suddenly there came from heaven," etc.] To them of old, no one "from heaven" appears, while they as yet follow after a vocation on earth; but now that Man has gone up on high, the Spirit also descends mightily from on high. "As it were a rushing mighty wind;" making it manifest by this, that nothing shall be able to withstand them, but they shall blow away all adversaries like a heap of dust. "And it filled all the house." The house also was a symbol of the world. "And it sat upon each of them," [etc.] and "the multitude came together, and were confounded." Observe their piety; they pronounce no hasty judgment, but are perplexed: whereas those reckless ones pronounce at once, saying, "These men are full of new wine." Now it was in order that they might have it in their power, in compliance with the Law, to appear thrice in the year in the Temple, that they dwelt there, these "devout men from all nations." Observe here, the writer has no intention of flattering them. For he does not say that they pronounced any opinion: but what? "Now when this was noised abroad, the multitude came together, and were confounded." And well they might be; for they supposed the matter was now coming to an issue against them, on account of the outrage committed against Christ. Conscience also agitated their souls, the very blood being yet upon their hands, and every thing alarmed them. "Behold, are not all these which speak Galileans?" For indeed this was confessed. ["And how hear we"] so much did the sound alarm them. ["Every man in our own tongue," etc.] for it found the greater part of the world assembled there. ["Parthians and Medes," etc.] This nerved the Apostles: for, what it was to speak in the Parthian tongue, they knew not but now learned from what those said. Here is mention made of nations that were hostile to them, Cretans, Arabians, Egyptians, Persians: and that they would conquer them all was here made manifest. But as to their being in those countries, they were there in captivity, many of them: or else, the doctrines of the Law had become disseminated [among] the Gentiles in those countries. So then the testimony comes from all quarters: from citizens, from foreigners, from proselytes. "We do hear them speak in our tongues the wonderful works of God." For it was not only that they spoke (in their tongues), but the things they spoke were wonderful. Well then might they be in doubt: for never had the like occurred. Observe the ingenuousness of these men. They were amazed and were in doubt, saying, "What means this?" But "others mocking said, 'These men are full of new wine'" (John viii. 48), and therefore mocked. O the effrontery! And what wonder is it? Since even of the Lord Himself, when casting out devils, they said that He had a devil! For so it is; wherever impudent assurance exists, it has but one object in view, to speak at all hazards, it cares not what; not that the man should say something real and relevant to the matter of discourse, but that he should speak no matter what. ["They are full of new wine."] Quite a thing of course (is not it?), that men in the midst of such dangers, and dreading the worst, and in such despondency, have the courage to utter such things! And observe: since this was unlikely; because they would not have been drinking much [at that early hour], they ascribe the whole matter to the quality (of the wine), and say, "They are full" of it. "But Peter, standing up with the eleven, lifted up his voice, and said unto them." In a former place you saw his provident forethought, here you see his manly courage. For if they were astonished and amazed, was it not as wonderful that he should be able in the midst of such a multitude to find language, he, an unlettered and ignorant man? If a man is troubled when he speaks among friends, much more might he be troubled among enemies and bloodthirsty men. That they are not drunken, he shows immediately by his very voice, that they are not beside themselves, as the soothsayers: and this too, that they were not constrained by some compulsory force. What is meant by, "with the eleven?" They expressed themselves through one common voice, and he was the mouth of all. The eleven stood by as witnesses to what he said. "He lifted up his voice," it is said. That is, he spoke with great confidence, that they might perceive the grace of the Spirit. He who had not endured the questioning of a poor girl, now in the midst of the people, all breathing murder, discourses with such confidence, that this very thing becomes an unquestionable proof of the Resurrection: in the midst of men who could deride and make a joke of such things as these! What effrontery, think you, must go to that! what impiety, what shamelessness! For wherever the Holy Spirit is present, He makes men of gold out of men of clay. Look, I pray you, at Peter now: examine well that timid one, and devoid of understanding; as Christ said, "Are ye also yet without understanding?" (Matt. xv. 16) the man, who after that marvellous confession was called "Satan." (xvi. 23.) Consider also the unanimity of the Apostles. They themselves ceded to him the office of speaking; for it was not necessary that all should speak. "And he lifted up his voice," and spoke out to them with great boldness. Such a thing it is to be a spiritual man! Only let us also bring ourselves into a state meet for the grace from above, and all becomes easy. For as a man of fire falling into the midst of straw would take no harm, but do it to others: not he could take any harm, but they, in assailing him, destroy themselves. For the case here was just as if one carrying hay should attack one bearing fire: even so did the Apostles encounter these their adversaries with great boldness.

For what did it harm them, though they were so great a multitude? Did they not spend all their rage? did they not turn the distress upon themselves? Of all mankind were ever any so possessed with both rage and terror, as those became possessed? Were they not in an agony, and were dismayed, and trembled? For hear what they say, "Do ye wish to bring this man's blood upon us?" (Acts v. 28.) Did they (the Apostles) not fight against poverty and hunger: against ignominy and infamy (for they were accounted deceivers): did they not fight against ridicule and wrath and mockery? — for in their case the contraries met: some laughed at them, others punished them; — were they not made a mark for the wrathful passions, and for the merriment, of whole cities? exposed to factions and conspiracies: to fire, and sword, and wild beasts? Did not war beset them from every quarter, in ten thousand forms? And were they any more affected in their minds by all these things, than they would have been at seeing them in a dream or in a picture? With bare body they took the field against all the armed, though against them all men had arbitrary power [against them, were]: terrors of rulers, force of arms, in cities and strong walls: without experience, without skill of the tongue, and in the condition of quite ordinary men, matched against juggling conjurors, against impostors, against the whole throng of sophists, of rhetoricians, of philosophers grown mouldy in the Academy and the walks of the Peripatetics, against all these they fought the battle out. And the man whose occupation had been about lakes, so mastered them, as if it cost him not so much ado as even a contest with dumb fishes: for just as if the opponents he had to outwit were indeed more mute than fishes, so easily did he get the better of them! And Plato, that talked a deal of nonsense in his day, is silent now, while this man utters his voice everywhere; not among his own countrymen alone, but also among Parthians, and Medes, and Elamites, and in India, and in every part of the earth, and to the extremities of the world. Where now is Greece, with her big pretentions? Where the name of Athens? Where the ravings of the philosophers? He of Galilee, he of Bethsaida, he, the uncouth rustic, has overcome them all. Are you not ashamed — confess it — at the very name of the country of him who has defeated you? But if you hear his own name too, and learn that he was called Cephas, much more will you hide your faces. This, this has undone you quite; because you esteem this a reproach, and account glibness of tongue a praise, and want of glibness a disgrace. You have not followed the road you ought to have chosen, but leaving the royal road, so easy, so smooth, you have trodden one rough, and steep, and laborious. And therefore you have not attained unto the kingdom of heaven.

Why then, it is asked, did not Christ exercise His influence upon Plato, and upon Pythagoras? Because the mind of Peter was much more philosophical than their minds. They were in truth children shifted about on all sides by vain glory; but this man was a philosopher, one apt to receive grace. If you laugh at these words, it is no wonder; for those aforetime laughed, and said, the men were full of new wine. But afterwards, when they suffered those bitter calamities, exceeding all others in misery; when they saw their city falling in ruins, and the fire blazing, and the walls hurled to the ground, and those manifold frantic horrors, which no one can find words to express, they did not laugh then. And you will laugh then, if you have the mind to laugh, when the time of hell is close at hand, when the fire is kindled for your souls. But why do I speak of the future? Shall I show you what Peter is, and what Plato, the philosopher? Let us for the present examine their respective habits, let us see what were the pursuits of each. The one wasted his time about a set of idle and useless dogmas, and philosophical, as he says, that we may learn that the soul of our philosopher becomes a fly. Most truly said, a fly! not indeed changed into one, but a fly must have entered upon possession of the soul which dwelt in Plato; for what but a fly is worthy of such ideas! The man was full of irony, and of jealous feelings against every one else, as if he made it his ambition to introduce nothing useful, either out of his own head or other people's. Thus he adopted the metempsychosis from another, and from himself produced the Republic, in which he enacted those laws full of gross turpitude. Let the women, he says, be in common, and let the virgins go naked, and let them wrestle before the eyes of their lovers, and let there also be common fathers, and let the children begotten be common. But with us, not nature makes common fathers, but the philosophy of Peter does this; as for that other, it made away with all paternity. For Plato's system only tended to make the real father next to unknown, while the false one was introduced. It plunged the soul into a kind of intoxication and filthy wallowing. Let all, he says, have intercourse with the women without fear. The reason why I do not examine the maxims of poets, is, that I may not be charged with ripping up fables. And yet I am speaking of fables much more ridiculous than even those. Where have the poets devised anything so portentous as this? But (not to enter into the discussion of his other maxims), what say you to these — when he equips the females with arms, and helmets, and greaves, and says that the human race has no occasion to differ from the canine! Since dogs, he says, the female and the male, do just the same things in common, so let the women do the same works as the men, and let all be turned upside down. For the devil has always endeavored by their means to show that our race is not more honorable than that of brutes; and, in fact, some have gone to such a pitch of absurdity, as to affirm that the irrational creatures are endued with reason. And see in how many various ways he has run riot in the minds of those men! For whereas their leading men affirmed that our soul passes into flies, and dogs, and brute creatures; those who came after them, being ashamed of this, fell into another kind of turpitude, and invested the brute creatures with all rational science, and made out that the creatures — which were called into existence on our account — are in all respects more honorable than we! They even attribute to them foreknowledge and piety. The crow, they say, knows God, and the raven likewise, and they possess gifts of prophecy, and foretell the future; there is justice among them, and polity, and laws. Perhaps you do not credit the things I am telling you. And well may you not, nurtured as you have been with sound doctrine; since also, if a man were fed with this fare, he would never believe that there exists a human being who finds pleasure in eating dung. The dog also among them is jealous, according to Plato. But when we tell them that these things are fables, and are full of absurdity, 'You do not enter into the higher meaning,' say they. No, we do not enter into this your surpassing nonsense, and may we never do so: for it requires (of course!) an excessively profound mind, to inform me, what all this impiety and confusion would be at. Are you talking, senseless men, in the language of crows, as the children are wont (in play)? For you are in very deed children, even as they. But Peter never thought of saying any of these things: he uttered a voice, like a great light shining out in the dark, a voice which scattered the mist and darkness of the whole world. Again, his deportment, how gentle it was, how considerate how far above all vainglory; how he looked towards heaven without all self-elation, and this, even when raising up the dead! But if it had come to be in the power of any one of those senseless people (in mere fantasy of course) to do anything like it, would he not straightway have looked for an altar and a temple to be reared to him, and have wanted to be equal with the gods? since in fact when no such sign is forthcoming, they are forever indulging such fantastic conceits. And what, pray you, is that Minerva of theirs, and Apollo, and Juno? They are different kinds of demons among them. And there is a king of theirs, who thinks fit to die for the mere purpose of being accounted equal with the gods. But not so the men here: no, just the contrary. Hear how they speak on the occasion of the lame man's cure. "You men of Israel, why look ye so earnestly on us, as though by our own power or holiness we had made him to walk? (ch. iii. 12.) We also are men of like passions with you. (Ibid. xiv. 14.) But with those, great is the self-elation, great the bragging; all for the sake of men's honors, nothing for the pure love of truth and virtue. For where an action is done for glory, all is worthless. For though a man possess all, yet if he have not the mastery over this (lust), he forfeits all claim to true philosophy, he is in bondage to the more tyrannical and shameful passion. Contempt of glory; this it is that is sufficient to teach all that is good, and to banish from the soul every pernicious passion. I exhort you therefore to use the most strenuous endeavors to pluck out this passion by the very roots; by no other means can you have good esteem with God, and draw down upon you the benevolent regard of that Eye which never sleeps. Wherefore, let us use all earnestness to obtain the enjoyment of that heavenly influence, and thus both escape the trial of present evils, and attain unto the future blessings, through the grace and loving-kindness of our Lord Jesus Christ, with Whom to the Father and the Holy Ghost be glory.

AUGUSTINE OF HIPPO (D. 430)

Augustine is one of the most prolific of the Church Fathers. His collected works including his theological orations, sermons, letters, and pastoral reflections take up several bookshelves in a library. He is remembered not only as a bishop and administrator of the Church but a true pastor, caring for his flock in Hippo and preaching the gospel of the Lord. There are numerous biographies about his life as well as his famous autobiography called *The Confessions* where he speaks about the spiritual life in general and his own personal journey to Christianity as well.

Augustine was born in north Africa to Patricius and Monica. His father Patricius was a local government official who was a pagan and Monica was a devout Christian who prayed for her son Augustine's conversion to the Christian faith. His father sent him to the north African city of Carthage where he studied law and rhetoric. He eventually fell into the heretical teachings of Manichesim which was taught by Mani. Manichesim was based on a gnostic teaching of duality that the flesh was bad and the spirit is good. Manicheism was very popular during this time and many priests and bishops had to fight against these false teachings. Eventually Augustine traveled to Rome where he met Ambrose, Bishop of Milan. Through many conversations with Ambrose, Augustine realized his errors and accepted to be baptized into the Christian faith. He was baptized sometime in great Lent in 387.

In 396, Augustine became the bishop of Hippo, a small city in North Africa where he served until his death in 438. Augustine lived an austere lifestyle choosing to live in a monastic community rather in a special bishop's residence. The monastic community revolved around regular hours of prayer, community work, and time for reading and contemplation. Eventually Augustine wrote down their way of life in the Monastic Rules which are still used today by the Augustinian Brothers who follow the Rule of St. Augustine in the Catholic Church.

As was stated previously, Augustine was a prolific orator and theologian. He delivered many sermons and theological orations in his cathedral. Like Leo, Augustine had a pastoral heart and his sermons reflect his devotion to the scriptures. Unfortunately many scholars have focused their attention more on his theological writings which are many, yet his commentaries on the scriptures are worth more research and study. His homilies on Matthew and on the other gospels show a connection between the gospels and daily life, looking to Jesus Christ as the supreme example of love.

For Further Reading:

Augustine of Hippo. *Confessions* Garry Wills (ed.) (NY: Penguin, 2006).

_____. *The Monastic Rules* (NY: New City Press, 2004).

Brown, Peter. *Augustine of Hippo Rev. Ed.* (Berkeley, The University of California Press, 2000).

O'Donnell, James J. *Augustine: A New Biography* (New York, Harper Perennial, 2005).

Wills, Garry. *Saint Augustine* (New York, Penguin, 1999).

Sermon on John 1:1–5

1. When I give heed to what we have just read from the apostolic lesson, that "the natural man perceives not the things which are of the Spirit of God," 1 Corinthians 2:14 and consider that in the present assembly, my beloved, there must of necessity be among you many natural men, who know only according to the flesh, and cannot yet raise themselves to spiritual understanding, I am in great difficulty how, as the Lord shall grant, I may be able to express, or in my small measure to explain, what has been read from the Gospel, "In the beginning was the Word, and the Word was with God, and the Word was God;" for this the natural man does not perceive. What then, brethren? Shall we be silent for this cause? Why then is it read, if we are to be silent regarding it? Or why is it heard, if it be not explained? And why is it explained, if it be not understood? And so, on the other hand, since I do not doubt that there are among your number some who can not only receive it when explained, but even understand it before it is explained, I shall not defraud those who are able to receive it, from fear of my words being wasted on the ears of those who are not able to receive it. Finally, there will be present with us the compassion of God, so that perchance there may be enough for all, and each receive what he is able, while he who speaks says what he is able. For to speak of the matter as it is, who is able? I venture to say, my brethren, perhaps not John himself spoke of the matter as it is, but even he only as he was able; for it was man that spoke of God, inspired indeed by God, but still man. Because he was inspired he said something; if he had not been inspired, he would have said nothing; but because a man inspired, he spoke not the whole, but what a man could he spoke.

2. For this John, dearly beloved brethren, was one of those mountains concerning which it is written: "Let the mountains receive peace for your people, and the hills righteousness." The mountains are lofty souls, the hills little souls. But for this reason do the mountains receive peace, that the hills may be able to receive righteousness. What

is the righteousness which the hills receive? Faith, for "the just does live by faith." The smaller souls, however, would not receive faith unless the greater souls, which are called mountains, were illuminated by Wisdom herself, that they may be able to transmit to the little ones what the little ones can receive; and the hills live by faith, because the mountains receive peace. By the mountains themselves it was said to the Church, "Peace be with you;" and the mountains themselves in proclaiming peace to the Church did not divide themselves against Him from whom they received peace, John 20:19 that truly, not feignedly, they might proclaim peace.

3. For there are other mountains which cause shipwreck, on which, if any one drive his ship, she is dashed to pieces. For it is easy, when land is seen by men in peril, to make a venture as it were to reach it; but sometimes land is seen on a mountain, and rocks lie hid under the mountain; and when any one makes for the mountain, he falls on the rocks, and finds there not rest, but wrecking. So there have been certain mountains, and great have they appeared among men, and they have created heresies and schisms, and have divided the Church of God; but those who divided the Church of God were not those mountains concerning which it is said, "Let the mountains receive peace for your people." For in what manner have they received peace who have severed unity?

4. But those who received peace to proclaim it to the people have made Wisdom herself an object of contemplation, so far as human hearts could lay hold on that which "eye has not seen, nor ear heard, neither has ascended into the heart of man." (1 Corinthians 2:9.) If it has not ascended into the heart of man, how has it ascended into the heart of John? Was not John a man? Or perhaps neither into John's heart did it ascend, but John's heart ascended into it? For that which ascends into the heart of man is from beneath, to man; but that to which the heart of man ascends is above, from man. Even so brethren, can it be said that, if it ascended into the heart of John (if in any way it can be said), it ascended into his heart in so far as he was not man. What means "was not man"? In so far as he had begun to be

an angel. For all saints are angels, since they are messengers of God. Therefore to carnal and natural men, who are not able to perceive the things that are of God, what says the apostle? "For whereas ye say, I am of Paul, I of Apollos, are you not men?" (1 Corinthians 3:4.) What did he wish to make them whom he upbraided because they were men? Do you wish to know what he wished to make them? Hear in the Psalms: "I have said, you are gods; and all of you are children of the Most High." To this, then, God calls us, that we be not men. But then will it be for the better that we be not men, if first we recognize the fact that we are men, that is, to the end that we may rise to that height from humility; lest, when we think that we are something when we are nothing, we not only do not receive what we are not, but even lose what we are.

5. Accordingly, brethren, of these mountains was John also, who said, "In the beginning was the Word, and the Word was with God, and the Word was God." This mountain had received peace; he was contemplating the divinity of the Word. Of what sort was this mountain? How lofty? He had risen above all peaks of the earth, he had risen above all plains of the sky, he had risen above all heights of the stars, he had risen above all choirs and legions of the angels. For unless he rose above all those things which were created, he would not arrive at Him by whom all things were made. You cannot imagine what he rose above, unless you see at what he arrived. Do you inquire concerning heaven and earth? They were made. Do you inquire concerning the things that are in heaven and earth? Surely much more were they made. Do you inquire concerning spiritual beings, concerning angels, archangels, thrones, dominions, powers, principalities? These also were made. For when the Psalm enumerated all these things, it finished thus: "He spoke, and they were made; He commanded, and they were created." If "He spoke and they were made," it was by the Word that they were made; but if it was by the Word they were made, the heart of John could not reach to that which he says, "In the beginning was the Word, and the Word was with God, and the Word was God," unless he had risen above all things that were made

by the Word. What a mountain this! How holy! How high among those mountains that received peace for the people of God, that the hills might receive righteousness!

6. Consider, then, brethren, if perchance John is not one of those mountains concerning whom we sang a little while ago, "I have lifted up my eyes to the mountains, from whence shall come my help." Therefore, my brethren, if you would understand, lift up your eyes to this mountain, that is, raise yourselves up to the evangelist, rise to his meaning. But, because though these mountains receive peace he cannot be in peace who places his hope in man, do not so raise your eyes to the mountain as to think that your hope should be placed in man; and so say, "I have lifted up my eyes to the mountains, from whence shall come my help," that you immediately add, "My help is from the Lord, who made heaven and earth." Therefore let us lift our eyes to the mountains, from whence shall come our help; and yet it is not in the mountains themselves that our hope should be placed, for the mountains receive what they may minister to us; therefore, from whence the mountains also receive there should our hope be placed. When we lift our eyes to the Scriptures, since it was through men the Scriptures were ministered, we are lifting our eyes to the mountains, from whence shall come our help; but still, since they were men who wrote the Scriptures, they did not shine of themselves, but "He was the true light, (John 1:9) who lights every man that comes into the world." A mountain also was that John the Baptist, who said, "I am not the Christ," (John 1:30) lest any one, placing his hope in the mountain, should fall from Him who illuminates the mountain. He also confessed, saying, "Since of His fullness have all we received." (John 1:16.) So you ought to say, "I have lifted up my eyes to the mountains, from whence shall come my help," so as not to ascribe to the mountains the help that comes to you; but continue and say, "My help is from the Lord, who made heaven and earth."

7. Therefore, brethren, may this be the result of my admonition, that you understand that in raising your hearts to the Scriptures (when the gospel was sounding forth, "In the beginning was the Word, and

the Word was with God, and the Word was God," and the rest that was read), you were lifting your eyes to the mountains. For unless the mountains said these things, you would not find out how to think of them at all. Therefore from the mountains came your help, that you even heard of these things; but you cannot yet understand what you have heard. Call for help from the Lord, who made heaven and earth; for the mountains were enabled only so to speak as not of themselves to illuminate, because they themselves are also illuminated by hearing. Thence John, who said these things, received them — he who lay on the Lord's breast, and from the Lord's breast drank in what he might give us to drink. But he gave us words to drink. You ought then to receive understanding from the source from which he drank who gave you to drink; so that you may lift up your eyes to the mountains from whence shall come your aid, so that from thence you may receive, as it were, the cup, that is, the word, given you to drink; and yet, since your help is from the Lord, who made heaven and earth, you may fill your breast from the source from which he filled his; whence you said, "My help is from the Lord, who made heaven and earth:" let him, then, fill who can. Brethren, this is what I have said: Let each one lift up his heart in the manner that seems fitting, and receive what is spoken. But perhaps you will say that I am more present to you than God. Far be such a thought from you! He is much more present to you; for I appear to your eyes, He presides over your consciences. Give me then your ears, Him your hearts, that you may fill both. Behold, your eyes, and those your bodily senses, you lift up to us; and yet not to us, for we are not of those mountains, but to the gospel itself, to the evangelist himself: your hearts, however, to the Lord to be filled. Moreover, let each one so lift up as to see what he lifts up, and whither. What do I mean by saying, "what he lifts up, and whither?" Let him see to it what sort of a heart he lifts up, because it is to the Lord he lifts it up, lest, encumbered by a load of fleshly pleasure, it fall ere ever it is raised. But does each one see that he bears a burden of flesh? Let him strive by continence to purify that which he may lift up to God. For "Blessed are the pure in heart, because they shall see God." (Matthew 5:8.)

8. But let us see what advantage it is that these words have sounded, "In the beginning was the Word, and the Word was with God, and the Word was God." We also uttered words when we spoke. Was it such a word that was with God? Did not those words which we uttered sound and pass away? Did God's Word, then, sound and come to an end? If so, how were all things made by it, and without it was nothing made? how is that which it created ruled by it, if it sounded and passed away? What sort of a word, then, is that which is both uttered and passes not away? Give ear, my beloved, it is a great matter. By everyday talk, words here become despicable to us, because through their sounding and passing away they are despised, and seem nothing but words. But there is a word in the man himself which remains within; for the sound proceeds from the mouth. There is a word which is spoken in a truly spiritual manner, that which you understand from the sound, not the sound itself. Mark, I speak a word when I say "God." How short the word which I have spoken — four letters and two syllables! Is this all that God is, four letters and two syllables? Or is that which is signified as costly as the word is paltry? What took place in your heart when you heard, "God"? What took place in my heart when I said "God"? A certain great and perfect substance was in our thoughts, transcending every changeable creature of flesh or of soul. And if I say to you, "Is God changeable or unchangeable?" you will answer immediately, "Far be it from me either to believe or imagine that God is changeable: God is unchangeable." Your soul, though small, though perhaps still carnal, could not answer me otherwise than that God is unchangeable: but every creature is changeable; how then were you able to enter, by a glance of your spirit, into that which is above the creature, so as confidently to answer me, "God is unchangeable"? What, then, is that in your heart, when you think of a certain substance, living, eternal, all-powerful, infinite, everywhere present, everywhere whole, nowhere shut in? When you think of these qualities, this is the word concerning God in your heart. But is this that sound which consists of four letters and two syllables? Therefore, whatever things are spoken and pass away

are sounds, are letters, are syllables. His word which sounds passes away; but that which the sound signified, and was in the speaker as he thought of it, and in the hearer as he understood it, that remains while the sounds pass away.

9. Turn your attention to that word. You can have a word in your heart, as it were a design born in your mind, so that your mind brings forth the design; and the design is, so to speak, the offspring of your mind, the child of your heart. For first your heart brings forth a design to construct some fabric, to set up something great on the earth; already the design is conceived, and the work is not yet finished: you see what you will make; but another does not admire, until you have made and constructed the pile, and brought that fabric into shape and to completion; then men regard the admirable fabric, and admire the design of the architect; they are astonished at what they see, and are pleased with what they do not see: who is there who can see a design? If, then, on account of some great building a human design receives praise, do you wish to see what a design of God is the Lord Jesus Christ, that is, the Word of God? Mark this fabric of the world. View what was made by the Word, and then you will understand what is the nature of the world. Mark these two bodies of the world, the heavens and the earth. Who will unfold in words the beauty of the heavens? Who will unfold in words the fruitfulness of the earth? Who will worthily extol the changes of the seasons? Who will worthily extol the power of seeds? You see what things I do not mention, lest in giving a long list I should perhaps tell of less than you can call up to your own minds. From this fabric, then, judge the nature of the Word by which it was made: and not it alone; for all these things are seen, because they have to do with the bodily sense. By that Word angels also were made; by that Word archangels were made, powers, thrones, dominions, principalities; by that Word were made all things. Hence, judge what a Word this is.

10. Perhaps some one now answers me, "Who so conceives this Word?" Do not then imagine, as it were, some paltry thing when you hear, "the Word," nor suppose it to be words such as you hear them

every day — "he spoke such words," "such words he uttered," "such words you tell me;" for by constant repetition the term *word* has become, so to speak, worthless. And when you hear, "In the beginning was the Word," lest you should imagine something worthless, such as you have been accustomed to think of when you were wont to listen to human words, hearken to what you must think of: "The Word was God."

11. Now some unbelieving Arian may come forth and say that "the Word of God was made." How can it be that the Word of God was made, when God by the Word made all things? If the Word of God was itself also made, by what other Word was *it* made? But if you say that there is a Word of the Word, I say, that by which *it* was made is itself the only Son of God. But if you do not say there is a Word of the Word, allow that that was not made by which all things were made. For that by which all things were made could not be made by itself. Believe the evangelist then. For he might have said, "In the beginning God made the Word:" even as Moses said, "In the beginning God made the heavens and the earth;" and enumerates all things thus: "God said, Let it be made, and it was made." (Genesis i.) If "said," who said? God. And what was made? Some creature. Between the speaking of God and the making of the creature, what was there by which it was made but the Word? For God said, "Let it be made, and it was made." This Word is unchangeable; although changeable things are made by it, the Word itself is unchangeable.

12. Do not then believe that that was made by which were made all things, lest you be not new-made by the Word, which makes all things new. For already have you been made by the Word, but it behoves you to be new-made by the Word. If, however, your belief about the Word be wrong, you will not be able to be new-made by the Word. And although creation by the Word has happened to you, so that you have been made by Him, you are unmade by yourself: if by yourself you are unmade, let Him who made you make you new: if by yourself you have been made worse, let Him who created you re-create you. But how can He re-create you by the Word, if you hold

a wrong opinion about the Word? The evangelist says, "In the beginning was the Word;" and you say, "In the beginning the Word was made." He says, "All things were made by Him;" and you say that the Word Himself was made. The evangelist might have said, "In the beginning the Word was made:" but what does he say? "In the beginning was the Word." If He was, He was not made; that all things might be made by it, and without Him nothing be made. If, then, "in the beginning the Word was, and the Word was with God, and the Word was God;" if you can not imagine what it is, wait till you are grown. That is strong meat: receive milk that you may be nourished, and be able to receive strong meat.

13. Give good heed to what follows, brethren, "All things were made by Him, and without Him was nothing made," so as not to imagine that "nothing" is something. For many, wrongly understanding "without Him was nothing made," are wont to fancy that "nothing" is something. Sin, indeed, was not made by Him; and it is plain that sin is nothing, and men become nothing when they sin. An idol also was not made by the Word; — it has indeed a sort of human form, but man himself was made by the Word; — for the form of man in an idol was not made by the Word, and it is written, "We know that an idol is nothing." (1 Corinthians 8:4.) Therefore these things were not made by the Word; but whatever was made in the natural manner, whatever belongs to the creature, everything that is fixed in the sky, that shines from above, that flies under the heavens, and that moves in universal nature, every creature whatsoever: I will speak more plainly, brethren, that you may understand me; I will say, from an angel even to a worm. What more excellent than an angel among created things? what lower than a worm? He who made the angel made the worm also; but the angel is fit for heaven, the worm for earth. He who created also arranged. If He had placed the worm in heaven, you might have found fault; if He had willed that angels should spring from decaying flesh, you might have found fault: and yet God almost does this, and He is not to be found fault with. For all men born of flesh, what are they but worms? and of these worms God

makes angels. For if the Lord Himself says, "But I am a worm and no man," who will hesitate to say what is written also in Job, "How much more is man rottenness, and the son of man a worm?" (Job 25:6.) First he said, "Man is rottenness;" and afterwards, "The son of man a worm:" because a worm springs from rottenness, therefore "man is rottenness," and "the son of man a worm." Behold what for your sake He was willing to become, who "in the beginning was the Word, and the Word was with God, and the Word was God!" Why did He for your sake become this? That you might suck, who were not able to chew. Wholly in this sense, then, brethren, understand "All things were made by Him, and without Him was nothing made." For every creature, great and small, was made by Him: by Him were made things above and things beneath; spiritual and corporeal, by Him were they made. For no form, no structure, no agreement of parts, no substance whatever that can have weight, number, measure, exists but by that Word, and by that Creator Word, to whom it is said, "You have ordered all things in measure, and in number, and in weight." (Wisdom 11:21.)

14. Therefore, let no one deceive you, when perchance you suffer annoyance from flies. For some have been mocked by the devil, and taken with flies. As fowlers are accustomed to put flies in their traps to deceive hungry birds, so these have been deceived with flies by the devil. Some one or other was suffering annoyance from flies; a Manichæan found him in his trouble, and when he said that he could not bear flies, and hated them exceedingly, immediately the Manichæan said, "Who made them?" And since he was suffering from annoyance, and hated them, he dared not say, "God made them," though he was a Catholic. The other immediately added, "If God did not make them, who made them?" "Truly," replied the Catholic, "I believe the devil made them." And the other immediately said, "If the devil made the fly, as I see you allow, because you understand the matter well, who made the bee, which is a little larger than the fly?" The Catholic dared not say that God made the bee and not the fly, for the case was much the same. From the bee he led him to the locust; from the

locust to the lizard; from the lizard to the bird; from the bird to the sheep; from the sheep to the cow; from that to the elephant, and at last to man; and persuaded a man that man was not made by God. Thus the miserable man, being troubled with the flies, became himself a fly, and the property of the devil. In fact, Beelzebub, they say, means "Prince of flies;" and of these it is written, "Dying flies deprive the ointment of its sweetness." (Ecclesiastes 10:1.)

15. What then, brethren? why have I said these things? Shut the ears of your hearts against the wiles of the enemy. Understand that God made all things, and arranged them in their orders. Why, then, do we suffer many evils from a creature that God made? Because we have offended God? Do angels suffer these things? Perhaps we, too, in that life of theirs, would have no such thing to fear. For your punishment, accuse your sin, not the Judge. For, on account of our pride, God appointed that tiny and contemptible creature to torment us; so that, since man has become proud and has boasted himself against God, and, though mortal, has oppressed mortals, and, though man, has not acknowledged his fellowman, — since he has lifted himself up, he may be brought low by gnats. Why are you inflated with human pride? Some one has censured you, and you are swollen with rage. Drive off the gnats, that you may sleep: understand who you are. For, that you may know, brethren, it was for the taming of our pride these things were created to be troublesome to us, God could have humbled Pharaoh's proud people by bears, by lions, by serpents; He sent flies and frogs upon them, (Exodus viii) that their pride might be subdued by the meanest creatures.

16. "All things," then, brethren, "all things were made by Him, and without Him was nothing made." But how were all things made by Him? "That, which was made, in Him is life." It can also be read thus: "That, which was made in Him, is life;" and if we so read it, everything is life. For what is there that was not made in Him? For He is the Wisdom of God, and it is said in the Psalm, "In Wisdom have You made all things." If, then, Christ is the Wisdom of God, and the Psalm says, "In Wisdom have You made all things:" as all things were made

by Him, so all things were made in Him. If, then, all things were made in Him, dearly beloved brethren, and that, which was made in Him, is life, both the earth is life and wood is life. We do indeed say wood is life, but in the sense of the wood of the cross, whence we have received life. A stone, then, is life. It is not seemly so to understand the passage, as the same most vile sect of the Manichæans creep stealthily on us again, and say that a stone has life, that a wall has a soul, and a cord has a soul, and wool, and clothing. For so they are accustomed to talk in their raving; and when they have been driven back and refuted, they in some sort bring forward Scripture, saying, "Why is it said, 'That, which was made in Him, is life'?" For if all things were made in Him, all things are life. Be not carried away by them; read thus "That which was made;" here make a short pause, and then go on, "in Him is life." What is the meaning of this? The earth was made, but the very earth that was made is not life; but there exists spiritually in the Wisdom itself a certain reason by which the earth was made: this is life.

17. As far as I can, I shall explain my meaning to you, beloved. A carpenter makes a box. First he has the box in design; for if he had it not in design, how could he produce it by workmanship? But the box in theory is not the very box as it appears to the eyes. It exists invisibly in design, it will be visible in the work. Behold, it is made in the work; has it ceased to exist in design? The one is made in the work, and the other remains which exists in design; for that box may rot, and another be fashioned according to that which exists in design. Give heed, then, to the box as it is in design, and the box as it is in fact. The actual box is not life, the box in design is life; because the soul of the artificer, where all these things are before they are brought forth, is living. So, dearly beloved brethren, because the Wisdom of God, by which all things have been made, contains everything according to design before it is made, therefore those things which are made through this design itself are not forthwith life, but whatever has been made is life in Him. You see the earth, there is an earth in design; you see the sky, there is a sky in design; you see the sun and

the moon, these also exist in design: but externally they are bodies, in design they are life. Understand, if in any way you are able, for a great matter has been spoken. If I am not great by whom it is spoken, or through whom it is spoken, still it is from a great authority. For these things are not spoken by me who am small; He is not small to whom I refer in saying these things. Let each one take in what he can, and to what extent he can; and he who is not able to take in any of it, let him nourish his heart, that he may become able. How is he to nourish it? Let him nourish it with milk, that he may come to strong meat. Let him not leave Christ born through the flesh till he arrive at Christ born of the Father alone, the God-Word with God, through whom all things were made; for that is life, which in Him is the light of men.

18. For this follows: "and the life was the light of men;" and from this very life are men illuminated. Cattle are not illuminated, because cattle have not rational minds capable of seeing wisdom. But man was made in the image of God, and has a rational mind, by which he can perceive wisdom. That life, then, by which all things were made, is itself the light; yet not the light of every animal, but of men. Wherefore a little after he says, "That was the true light, which lights every man that comes into the world." By that light John the Baptist was illuminated; by the same light also was John the Evangelist himself illuminated. He was filled with that light who said, "I am not the Christ; but He comes after me, whose shoe's latchet I am not worthy to unloose." (John 1;26–27.) By that light he had been illuminated who said, "In the beginning was the Word, and the Word was with God, and the Word was God." Therefore that life is the light of men.

19. But perhaps the slow hearts of some of you cannot yet receive that light, because they are burdened by their sins, so that they cannot see. Let them not on that account think that the light is in any way absent, because they are not able to see it; for they themselves are darkness on account of their sins. "And the light shines in darkness, and the darkness comprehended it not." Accordingly, brethren, as in the case of a blind man placed in the sun, the sun is present to him, but he is absent from the sun. So every foolish man, every unjust

man, every irreligious man, is blind in heart. Wisdom is present; but it is present to a blind man, and is absent from his eyes; not because it is absent from him, but because he is absent from it. What then is he to do? Let him become pure, that he may be able to see God. Just as if a man could not see because his eyes were dirty and sore with dust, rheum, or smoke, the physician would say to him: "Cleanse from your eye whatever bad thing is in it, so that you may be able to see the light of your eyes." Dust, rheum, and smoke are sins and iniquities: remove then all these things, and you will see the wisdom that is present; for God is that wisdom, and it has been said, "Blessed are the pure in heart; for they shall see God." (Matthew 5:8.)

ABOUT THE AUTHOR

Fr. William Mills, Ph.D. is the rector of the Nativity of the Holy Virgin Orthodox Church in Charlotte, NC, as well as an adjunct professor of religious studies at Queens University in Charlotte, NC. Fr. Mills received his Bachelor of History from Millersville University of Pennsylvania and then pursued theological studies at Saint Vladimir's Theological Orthodox Seminary in Crestwood, NY where he received both a Master of Divinity and Master of Theology degrees. He then pursued advanced theological studies at the Union Institute and University in Cincinnati, Ohio where he received his doctorate in Pastoral Theology. Fr. Mills is available for parish and clergy retreats. He is also a founding member of the Orthodox Center for the Advancement of Biblical Studies (www.ocabs.org). You can also visit his personal website at www.wcmills.com.

Printed in the United States
123222LV00004B/34/P